CW01262923

MG
T SERIES
In Detail

MG
T SERIES

In Detail

TA - TF 1935-55

BY PADDY WILLMER

Herridge & Sons

Published in 2005 by
Herridge & Sons Ltd
Lower Forda, Shebbear,
Beaworthy, Devon EX21 5SY

Reprinted 2012

© Copyright Paddy Willmer 2005

Designed by Jonathan Davison
Special photography by Simon Clay

All rights reserved. No part of this publication may be reproduced in any form or by any means without the prior permission of the publisher.

ISBN 978-0-954106-36-2
Printed in China

Picture Acknowledgments
The author and the publisher are grateful to the MG Car Club, the T-Register and its members for supplying photographs:

Contents

Introduction	6
Company History	8
The TA	14
The TB	48
The TC	66
The TD	90
The TF	112
T-type Racing	136
Evolution of a Racer	148
Tuning	162
Appendices	167

Introduction

I am conscious that a book of this nature, produced 50 years after these cars ceased production, cannot be anything other than multi-authored. When you consider how many books have been written about them already, together with all the workshop manuals, magazine articles and owner's club publications, this can be no more than a distillation. However, I have endeavoured to cast a fresh light on these cars from my personal experience of 43 years' ownership, 40-odd years of racing T-types, 30 years of driving a TB on the road, and some of what I have already written in MG Car Club T Register publications.

For help in this task I would particularly single out the New England MG T Register Handbook, Mike Sherrell's seminal work *TCs Forever*, Chris Harvey's *Immortal T Series*, and the Owner's Handbooks and Workshop Manuals of the various models. Gregor Grant's *British Sports Cars*, the W E Blower MG Workshop Manual and Autobook Workshop Manuals also provided a lot of guidance. There are several drawings in this book which have never been seen in one place before, and many of the photographs, a large amount from my own collection, will be new to you.

I would like to thank members of the T Register for their help, especially David Butler, Peter Jones, Ken Selby and Julian White, for the use of their cars, and others for reminding me of things and pointing me in the right direction.

I am indebted to the MG Car Club for the loan of many photographs and for being a mentor and supporter for very many years. For the camaraderie, friendship, fun and larking about with my T Racing colleagues, nothing can be said other than that those were the days of my life!

I would also like to thank Hilary Martin for all her help in transcribing my chaotic manuscripts. Finally, I would like to dedicate this book to my wife, Helen, and to daughters Chloe and Elizabeth, who support and care for me, as well as to the memory of my old friend and racing colleague, Malcolm Hogg, who so sadly died just before it was to be published.

This is the story of arguably the longest-lasting family of cars of the MG Car Company – longest lasting not only in their longevity but also in that they were in production for 19 years, though one could reduce this figure by six years due to World War II. One could caution against that, as even in those dark days there were fresh thoughts in the minds of those whose work was temporarily diverted into producing tanks and aeroplanes.

The MG T-types, from TA to TF, were to influence hundreds of thousands of people, to mould their lives, careers and aspirations, and they continue to do so to this day.

They started the import revolution in a then isolationist United States of America, they won Grand Prix in Australia, and later created long-distance touring records there and worldwide. In South Africa they followed in the footsteps of the Boer trekkers, covering vast distances. One TA actually drove all the way from London to Cape Town when no roads existed for hundreds of miles. They became the property of the rich and famous and even of royalty. They are equally at home on wide boulevards, twisty mountain lanes, muddy hillsides, shingle tracks and full-blown racetracks. Wherever they park crowds gather, just as they did when they were new.

I first became entranced by the MG T-type at the age of seven when, walking back from school on a sunny afternoon, I heard a rasping noise behind me and saw a beautiful little car being driven by a policeman – it was in fact a police car – coming towards me along the road. As it passed and went away up the hill the sun caught the wheel spinners and they sparkled. It was the most beautiful thing I had ever seen. Of course I was a young child and soon forgot it, but I must have filed this vision away in the back of my mind because 10 years later or so, when I was listening to Le Mans clandestinely under the bedclothes on a small radio, I dreamed of becoming a racing driver and rushing through the night like the heroes of those times. Then as I got a little bit older and passed my driving test I was thinking of what sort of car I would like; unbidden, the MG that I had seen years earlier leapt into my mind and I thought, that's it, that's what I want.

I made a false start with a BSA Scout wearing an Aston Martin DB3S body, but traded that in for an MG TA that I saw in a garage in Cambridge. The year was 1961 and the car cost me £65. That was the beginning and I have never been without a T-type MG to this day. I relinquished the TA in October 1962 and bought a TC because that model, as you will learn from this book, has a completely different engine from the TA, a much more robust one, which would suit me as I fancied going racing. I sold the TA to a couple of Italian students for the grand sum of £95 and paid £100 for the TC. I never saw the TA again but the TC then launched me on a competition career which started in July 1963 at the Firle Hill climb near Lewes in Sussex and ended in 2002 at Silverstone. In between we competed all over the country at all the well-known circuits as well as in hillclimbs and sprints. With the same car I have won the drivers championship of the MG Car Club T Register, various class and special awards, first places in several races, seconds and thirds in others, and had a glorious time.

In 1975 I rolled the car at Cadwell Park and was faced with replacing the chassis, so I transplanted the whole works on to a TA chassis and the TC became a bit of a mongrel after that. Then in 1993 at Silverstone I had another major accident when I went into the side of a spinning car at Copse Corner. This split the chassis in half longitudinally. I had the car straightened out and rebuilt by Len Bull in Essex, and carried on racing until I decided that it was getting far too expensive. My last event was at Silverstone in 2001. I sold the car a little later to a fellow racer, and it is continuing its competition career even if I am not.

In the meantime I had also been a founder member of the MG Car Club T register and written in its bulletin, being editor from 1966 to 1969 and again from 1980 to 2001. I was also editor of the MG Car Club's main magazine *Safety Fast!* from 1985 to 2001, some sixteen years - the longest, I think, that anyone has ever held that position.

In 1968 I bought a second T-type, a TB, in a very poor state of repair. I had heard about it through some sort of grapevine and hurried off to see it as the owner was emigrating to the United States the following day (the car would have been scrapped if it hadn't been bought by me). It was a non-runner and cost me £20. By 1972 I had done enough work to get the car running and since that time it has undergone a trickle restoration with bigger and bigger engines and more of the redundant equipment off my racing car going into it. I also put it on 16-inch wheels. The original wings had rotted through so I fitted the front wings off my TC when I changed the TC racer over to cycle wings. A pair of new TC wings went on at the back, donated by a friend, and the TB is now a very solid little car, with a lot of timber replaced and a 1370cc engine which provides extra propulsion.

At the same time as this car came into my life I also bought a TC from a taxi driver in Cambridge. It was one T too many, so I had to sell it soon after. I think I doubled my money: £50 out and £100 in. Then in 1981 I found another. It was absolutely as it had come out of the factory. When I sold it, it paid for a new kitchen. The new owner is still rebuilding it some 20 years later. It is questionable that it needed a rebuild as with a new engine and radiator it was as new then!

As you will see, the TA, TB and TC, although looking very alike, are all very different cars, possibly more so than the TD and TF which followed.

Paddy Willmer.
August 2004

Chapter One

Company History

Two people were primarily responsible for the growth of the MG Car Company during the years between World War I and World War II.

First was Cecil Kimber, artist and engineer, who built and designed (in that order) the first Morris specials, which evolved into MG cars during the middle to late 1920s. He was then working for car manufacturer William Morris and had an intuitive knowledge of what the public wanted – or those members of the public who wanted something different from the bland uniformity in their lives. Kimber appreciated symmetry, and this led to his adoption of the octagon symbol with the letters MG in it to form the badge that is now so familiar to motorists the world over. It was his genius that spawned the series of big cars, the 14/40 and 18/80 in particular, which were developments of Morris models. During the 1930s, MG's and Morris's businesses and cars were entwined. Without the money and resources provided by William Morris, later Lord Nuffield, the early MGs and then the brilliant series of sports cars, sports-racing cars, racing cars and record breakers which followed would never have seen the light of day.

The first MG Midget, the M-type of 1929-32. This is a very early example with rear-hinged doors.

COMPANY HISTORY

In the first half of the 1930s Kimber produced the little M-Type, the J- and P-Type Midgets which were the forerunners of the T series, all of them powered by versions of Morris/Wolseley overhead-camshaft engines. He designed all these cars. The MG Car Company moved to Abingdon in the early 1930s and became semi-independent of William Morris, though he controlled the purse strings. Kimber must have had a lovely time designing all these models, seeing them race and break land speed records around the world, while prestigious races such as the Mille Miglia and the Tourist Trophy also fell to MGs. He even went on to design and have built the single-seater R-Type, whose chassis layout pre-dated that of the Lotus Elan by 35 years.

A major change in circumstances came in 1935, however, when Lord Nuffield withdrew all his support from racing and record breaking: MG, if it was to survive, henceforth would have to accept the dictates of Cowley and use components from the Morris Motors range of cars.

Before all of this happened another man came into the life of MG who was to direct its commercial success, both at home and worldwide, from 1931 to 1980. In my view he was the real architect of the fortunes of MG cars and, when Kimber was downcast by the 1935 ultimatum, picked up the pieces and made certain that future MG models would be successful, not only in the competition world, but more importantly, in the commercial world. This man was John Thornley, who joined the MG Car Company in 1931. He was initially hired on the one hand to assist with sales, and on the other to develop the MG Car Club that he had been instrumental in forming that year. Not an easy

William Morris, later Lord Nuffield, stands proudly alongside the MG K3 which won the 1933 Ulster TT driven by Nuvolari.

The J4 Midget of 1932, built for competition, had a supercharged version of the 746cc overhead-camshaft engine producing in excess of 70bhp.

In the lines of the PA Midget of 1934 can be seen the genesis of the T-type body style.

COMPANY HISTORY

Photographed in the late 1930s, Cecil Kimber (seated, fourth from left), with John Thornley on his left in the pale suit and other members of the Abingdon workforce.

job! By 1936, when the TA arrived, he was firmly established as the Company's Commercial Manager, and up to 1939, and then from 1945 to the late 1970s, he was the man whose efforts meant that, from the TA onwards, production figures of each subsequent sports model – apart from the short-lived TB and the limited runs of the MGC and MGB GT V8 – increased exponentially, from 3000 TAs to just over half a million MGBs when the Abingdon factory closed in 1980.

In the aftermath of Nuffield's edict a whole new breed of MGs was developed using components from the Morris Motors range, with engines from the group's standardised line-up, which was no longer to include the overhead-camshaft units so suuccessfully adopted by MG. The first of these new models was the 2-litre SA, produced 1935-1939. The engine was a six-cylinder pushrod ohv unit derived from the Wolseley 16hp, with a capacity of 2062cc and an output of 67bhp, but it was soon enlarged to 2288cc, lifting output to around 75bhp. The SA was the first MG to incorporate hydraulic braking.

In 1937 it was joined by the smaller VA, which again inherited a Morris/Wolseley engine. This one, based on the four-cylinder Wolseley 12/48 unit, had a capacity of 1549cc with a 69.5mm bore and the famous 102mm stroke, shared with the SA, that dated back to the Bullnose Morris. In MG form it produced 54bhp as against the Wolseley's 44bhp. The VA had a dry clutch inherited from the 12hp Morris and Wolseley models, although early cars had wet clutches which, as we will see, the TA also adopted. Later VA engines with the dry clutch revved considerably more freely, and several VA engines were to appear in T-types in years to come. Production of the VA lasted until 1939.

In 1938 the SA and VA were joined by the enormous WA, which featured a 2.6-litre 104bhp engine, this capacity being gained by boring out the SA engine to 2561cc, with a 73mm bore and the 102mm stroke. It introduced a counterbalanced crankshaft and thin-wall, steel-backed, white-metal shell bearings.

Like the engines in what is known as the SVW range, all future MG engines apart from Twin Cam MGAs were to incorporate pushrod-operated overhead valves. Thus the stage was set for the first of the pushrod-engined MG sports cars to succeed the J-Type and P-Type overhead camshaft models of the previous era, and more significantly, the Q-Type.

The 2.6-litre WA was the largest of the pre-war MGs designed by Kimber. This is a 1938 drophead coupe.

11

Forty-plus years of MG history outside the old Abingdon factory

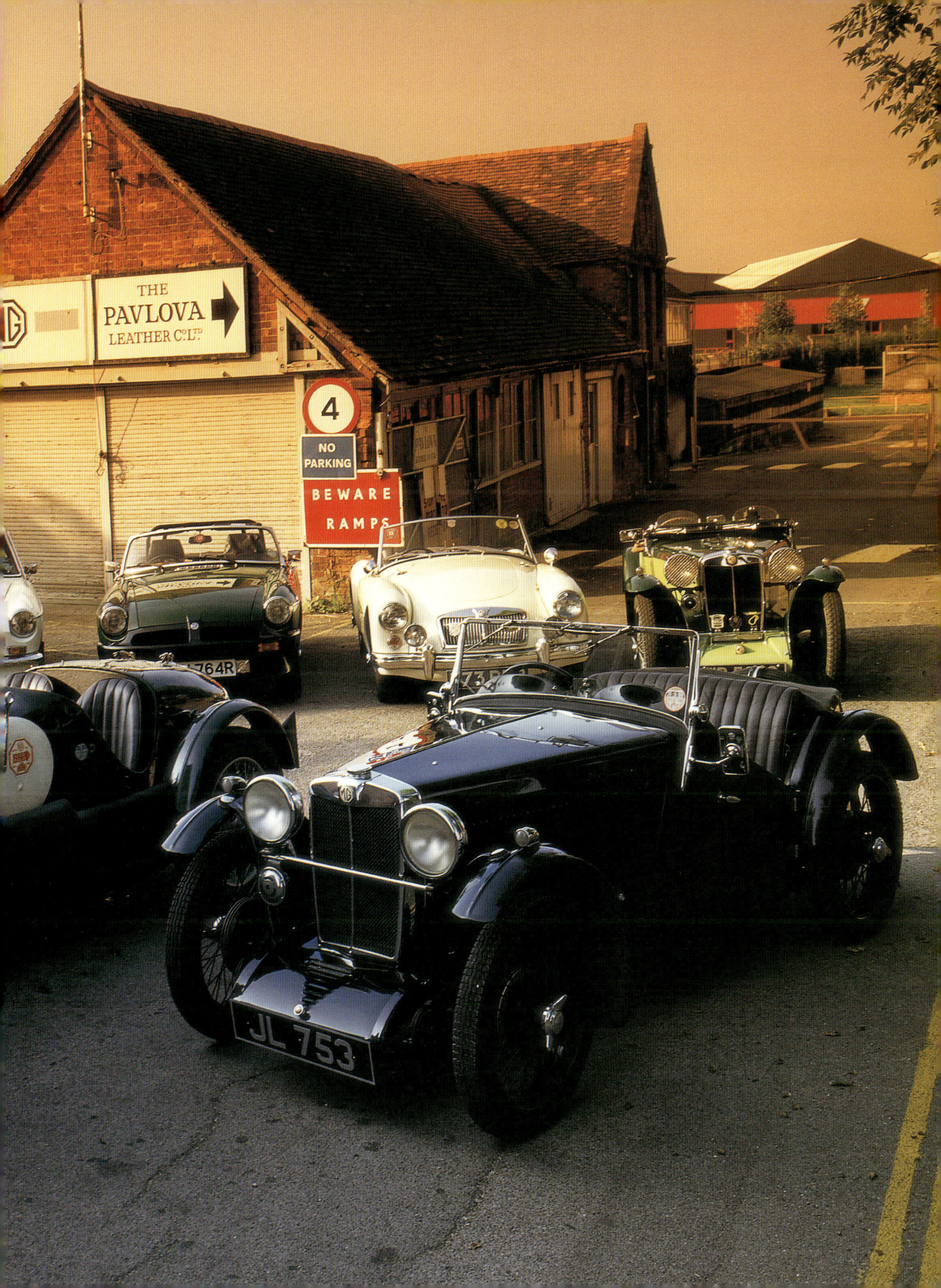
THE
PAVLOVA
LEATHER C^O.L^TD
4
NO
PARKING
BEWARE
RAMPS
JL 753

Chapter Two

The TA

By the time the TA was launched MG had pretty much perfected the style of their sports cars. It did not change significantly until the arrival of the TD model.

On 19 June 1936 the MG T-type was announced to the world. It was the first of a new series of MGs that was to last into the 1950s. It certainly looked traditionally MG, following on in the style of the P-type Midget it replaced, if a little larger. The big departure from all previous MG sports cars was its adoption of a pushrod engine in place of the earlier cars' Wolseley-derived overhead-camshaft units. MG enthusiasts of the time must have seen this as a retrograde step, but it was an unavoidable part of Lord Nuffield's rationalisation programme.

So the TA, as it was later renamed, broke new ground. It lost the rortiness of the J- and P-types. It acquired a wider body, its springs were "softer" – that is a very relative expression – and it drove completely differently. It met with deri-

The TA's rear window would originally have been split vertically, but this single-panel version is rather more practical. Note the boot rack.

sion from diehard enthusiasts, but gradually wooed the sports car public by appealing to a much wider cross-section of society. The TA was also a much heavier car than the P-type and Q-type it replaced, but the good torque characteristics of its long stroke-engine, despite its modest bhp, gave it a performance as good as, if not superior to, the P-type's.

The T-type inherited the track and wheelbase of the Q-type MG, that very fast supercharged mini-K3, so it had a track of 3ft 9in and a wheelbase of 7ft 10in.

A ladder chassis, boxed to its middle, with four crossmembers, formed its main structure. It was underslung at the rear, so the chassis ran under the back axle, and it was virtually straight apart from the front dumb irons. Suspension was via semi-elliptic leaf springs front and rear, with Luvax hydraulic lever arm shock absorbers. The back ends of both front and rear springs run in sliding trunnions, replaced later on the TC by conventional shackles.

The design of the chassis, with boxing only at the front end, means that roadholding is aided by the flexing of the chassis at the back, and the use of ash body construction aids the way the car handles by adjusting and limiting the flex of the chassis. Anyone who has driven a TA, TB or TC will know about this, especially when driving on uneven surfaces. However, these beam-axle, cart-sprung cars do arguably provide superior cornering on a smooth surface than the later cars with independent front suspension.

Roger Bragger's TA is a very early example, chassis number TA 0418 first registered in September 1936.

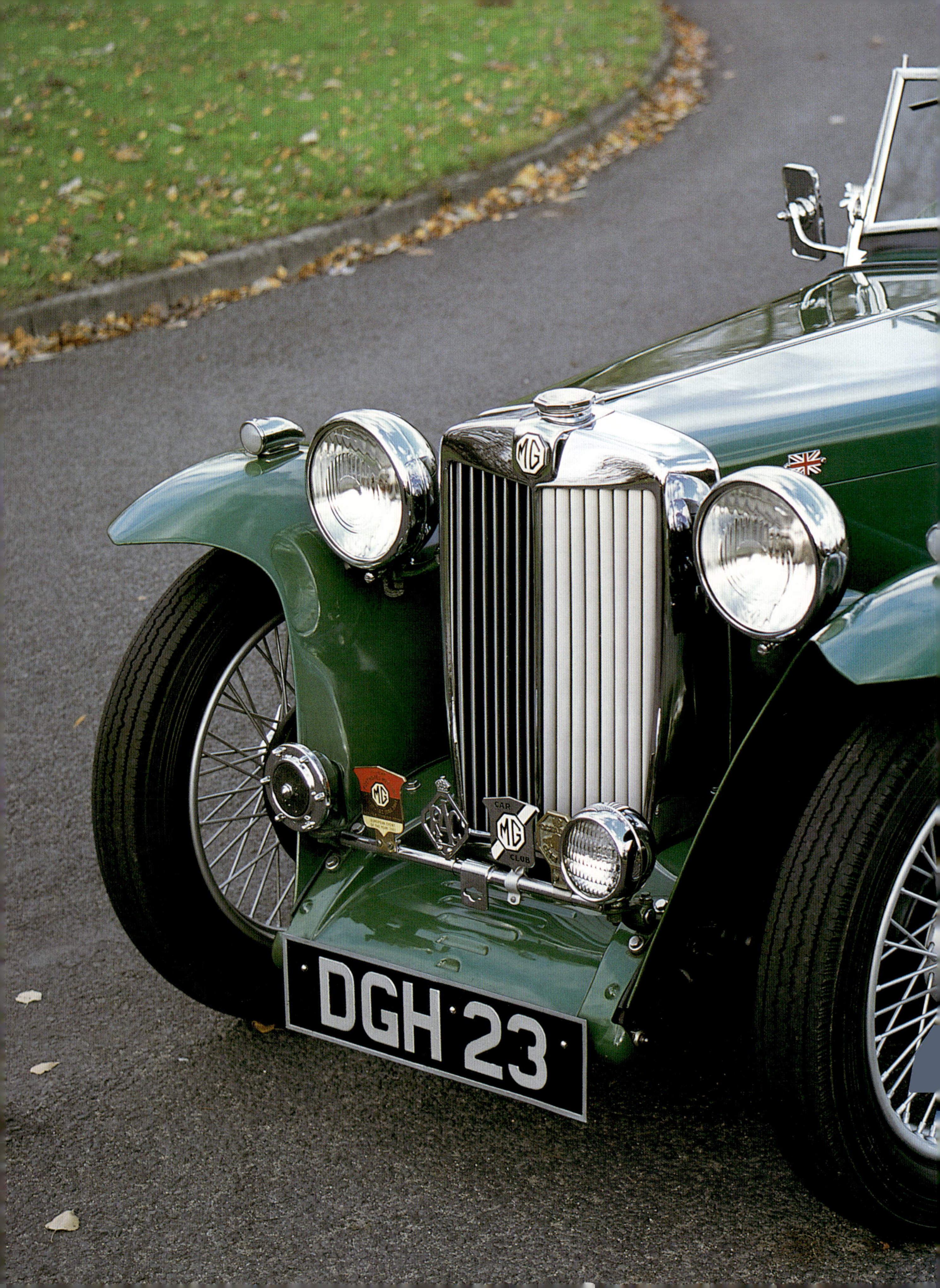
DGH 23

The horn and foglamp positions would remain the same through to the end of TC production, though this fog lamp is not of the original type.

The simple ladder chassis of the TA with its five main cross-members. The hidden one is underneath the radiator, which is fixed to it by two studs. You can see the battery cradles clearly. There is also a clear view of the way the brake lines are laid.

We shall see this when discussing the competition use of these cars later on.

The wheels were of the Rudge-Whitworth central locking type, made by Dunlop, and were of 19in diameter and had 48 spokes. The tyres were of 4.50 section. For competition work 16in wheels could be had as an optional extra.

The steering box is of the Bishop Cam design, where the bottom of the column is fitted with a spiral worm in which a peg fitted to the top of the rocker shaft rides. The rocker shaft is splined on to the drop arm with a pinch bolt. Adjustment to the rocker shaft is by shims inserted underneath the side plate, which in the TA/B and C is on the top of the box. This box was designed to fit other cars that had different steering arrangements and on the MG the rocker shaft would have stuck out sideways, so the box had to be fitted on its side. Fortunately this makes adjustment much easier. Column end float is adjusted by shims at both ends of the worm. These rarely need any adjustment, but by careful fine-tuning of the rocker shims it is possible to achieve the minimum play at the steering wheel (1 inch) and to be able to rotate the steering, with the wheels off the ground, smoothly over its one and a half turns lock to lock with no sticking in the central position. The steering box is oil tight – supposedly – and lubricated by EP140 oil, never grease, as this solidifies and ceases to lubricate the moving parts.

This steering box is vilified by a lot of modern day users, who often convert their cars by fitting steering boxes from Datsuns and VWs. They blame their cars' "bad steering" on the box. By bad steering, they mean wandering and bump-steer reaction. The steering may be stiff and there may be excessive play. In order to get a TA, B or C to steer properly one needs to achieve a combination of everything working in the same direction. Make sure the box is adjusted properly as already described. There must be no wear in the rocker shaft. The drop arm must be centered and bolted securely to the rocker shaft. The drag link must be adjusted properly. The drag link and track rod ends are adjustable. They are in a housing with two spring-loaded pads each side of the steering ball and are adjustable in quarter turns by a nut with a four-way split-pin adjustment. Fully tighten each joint by removing the split pin and adjusting with a large screwdriver. After the joint is fully tightened back it off a quarter turn. If it is still too tight, back it off one more until it feels free with no slop in it. Once you have done this, make sure the steering arms are firmly bolted and locked on to the brake back plate.

Even doing all this won't guarantee perfect steering. The chassis must be absolutely straight. The springs must be correctly cambered and be fixed firmly. On the TA and TB this means no wear in the trunnions or their housings, and accurate fit on the pins at the front of each spring. On the TC all the bushes and shackles must be tight. Make sure the front suspension is "toed" properly:

The 19-inch silver-painted Dunlop wheels have 48 spokes, and on early TAs they were laced on the outside of the rim, as here. Later cars had centre-laced wheels.

a toe-in of ⅛in at the front is usual.

The camber and caster angles must also be correct. Quite often you will see a car with an upright offside wheel and a positively-cambered nearside wheel. This means that the front axle is bent. Make sure the axle is fitted correctly, so that the kingpins lean back. The kingpins and their cotter pins must be tight, with minimal wear, and the hub bearings in the wheels should be correctly adjusted.

Steering is also affected by the rear of the car. Make sure that the axle is bolted securely to the springs and that the springs, trunnions and the housings are all fitting well. Many TAs and TBs have very thin and worn rear trunnion housings which eventually can break, with disastrous consequences. It is possible to obtain spare ends of the rear crossmember to renew the trunnion housings.

If you observe all this your TA, TB and TC will steer and handle like a dream. The writer's TB has always been blessed this way and can be steered with one finger on all but the most bumpy of roads. On a straight, smooth carriageway it will steer straight on with hands off the wheel, and will even follow its line through gradual curves following the road camber with no assistance from me. Achieve that, and you will be able to detect wear taking place very early on or prevent it. Until its steering is sorted out you will never be able to enjoy your car. Afterwards you can race, trial, drive it at 70mph on motorways, park it, gymkhana it, sprint it, hill climb it and it will never bite you back.

On the TA and TB the trunnions need lubricating every 500 miles. Use EP140 oil again, not grease. Most TAs and TBs have a central chassis lubrication system, consisting of three nipples on a plate on each side of the bulkhead. These

Side shot of the TA chassis gives a good view of the engine with its three-branch exhaust manifold and rearward facing air cleaner.

The TA with hood and side screens in position. The side screen is hinged to allow hand signals.

Factory shot in 1936 of CJO 617, a prototype TA, chassis number TA0252. You can clearly see the three running board strips, the rounded front edge to the front wings, the one-piece seat back and the standard tonneau cover, which only covered the space behind the seats.

From the same set of photographs, the rear view showing the slab tank, tiny single rear lamp (replaced by a larger lamp in 1937), twin-humped scuttle, flat-spoked steering wheel, external rear-view mirror.

With hood erected and side screens in position the TA still looks very neat.

A steering worm showing signs of serious wear, probably from lack of lubrication or from the use of grease instead of the correct 140-grade gear oil.

are connected by pipes to the front trunnion housing, the handbrake cables and the rear trunnion housings. Use an oil gun on these until resistance is felt and then up to 25 strokes for the trunnions, and five or six for the handbrake, will distribute the oil to the right spots. You know when to stop when the oil starts to leak out of the bottom of the trunnions. Avoid concrete drives when carrying this out, or even parking on one for up to 100 miles afterwards!

The TA's engine was coded MPJG (M for Morris, P for pushrod, J for 63.5mm bore, G for MG) and was based on the Wolseley 10/40, itself a version of the Morris 10/4 unit. The capacity was 1292cc, the bore 63.5mm (a classic Morris/BMC dimension found in a range of its engines) and the stroke 102mm again. This was very long but quite usual at the time due to the iniquitous RAC horsepower rating system inflicted by pre-war governments. The engine used up-to-date aluminium split-skirt pistons, initially with four rings, followed in later cars by three-ring solid skirt Aerolite pistons. The crankshaft had three 52mm white-metal main bearings and 45mm big-end journals. The connecting rods were 190mm centre to centre with white metal bearings. With its 6.5:1 compression ratio, the engine produced 50bhp at 4500rpm and, for such a small unit, a considerable amount of torque.

The camshaft sat in the left-hand side of the block and was driven by chain from the front of the crankshaft. It provided conservative valve timing of 11 degrees BTDC and 59 degrees ABDC on the inlet valves, and 56 degrees and 24 degrees respectively on the exhaust. It actuated the valves by pushrods set in camshaft lifters that rested in separate blocks of four accessed by twin apertures in the block, hidden by an outside tappet cover. These opened the valves via rockers running on a shaft supported by three pedestals bolted to the top of the cylinder head. The inlet valves were 30.5mm in diameter, the exhaust valves 26mm, and they had a 10mm lift. Early valve spring pressures were 60lb shut

MG T SERIES IN DETAIL

The author's 1937 TA in Wales in 1961. You can see the narrow, rather flimsy rear wing. Ten years earlier, in the hands of Paul Linney, it had competed in the national Daily Express Rally that in later years grew into the RAC Rally.

The author's TA again, a year later in 1962, in company with a Singer Nine. Both cars posessed a similar performance then.

and 108.5lb open (later 101lb shut, 170lb open). Triple valve springs were fitted.

The cast iron cylinder head had siamesed inlet ports, with separate exhaust ports for the front and rear cylinders and a central siamesed exhaust port. Carburation was by twin 1in semi-downdraught SUs using a standard 0.90 jet with a normal AC needle, richer and weaker needles being M1 and No 5 respectively. Some of the early carburettors had bronze bodies. They were bolted to a cast iron inlet manifold clamped to the head with four studs and bridging clamps. The cast iron three-branch exhaust manifold was joined to its downpipe by a three bolt-triangulated flange and an asbestos copper gasket. This became a frequent cause of failure, not only on this engine but on subsequent XPAG engines to be introduced later.

The water pump was driven by a belt that also drove the dynamo. This is quite a long belt as the pump is bolted to the front of the cylinder head high up on the engine on the TA, unlike later engines where it is bolted to the block. It might be as a result of this long belt run that TA water pumps were, and are, prone to premature failure. The bearing wears, causing run-out of the impeller, which then damages the sealing gland, leading to a major water leak.

Under the bonnet at the top of the bulkhead is the tool box, operated by catches each side, in the top of which sat tool trays with a larger space below for essential spares, and the jack. The SU fuel pump is mounted on the front of the offside toolbox and the coil is fitted in the horizontal position low down on the left side of the bulkhead. The control box and fusebox are mounted on the side of the nearside toolbox. The wiring loom is distributed from the control box to the instruments on the dashboard including the four-way dynamo/lights switch and the ammeter.

The ignition is by conventional coil and distributor. The distributor is mounted on the nearside of the block and driven by a geared shaft meshing with gears in the camshaft. The firing order was 1342.

Contact breaker points are set at 0.010-0.012in and timing is TDC. The rocker clearances are 0.010in on the inlet valves (hot) and 0.015in exhaust. It must be borne in mind that at this time fuel octane ratings were around 70. These days with octane ratings being between 95 and 99 the ignition can be advanced by at least 5 degrees.

The TA had a 12-volt electrical system, with 6-volt batteries in wells on either side of the propeller shaft ahead of the rear axle. They were charged by a three-brush dynamo, quite a substantial unit, fitted to the nearside of the engine and driven by a belt from the crankshaft pulley. The three-brush system is controlled from the dashboard by setting a high or low charge. The third brush was movable so that an accurate charging rate could

The identification plates on the front of the left-hand toolbox, and the body number plate on the sloping part of the scuttle.

Tools were stored in moulded rubber trays in top the toolbox on each side of the bulkhead. The trays lifted out to give access to spares and other tools underneath.

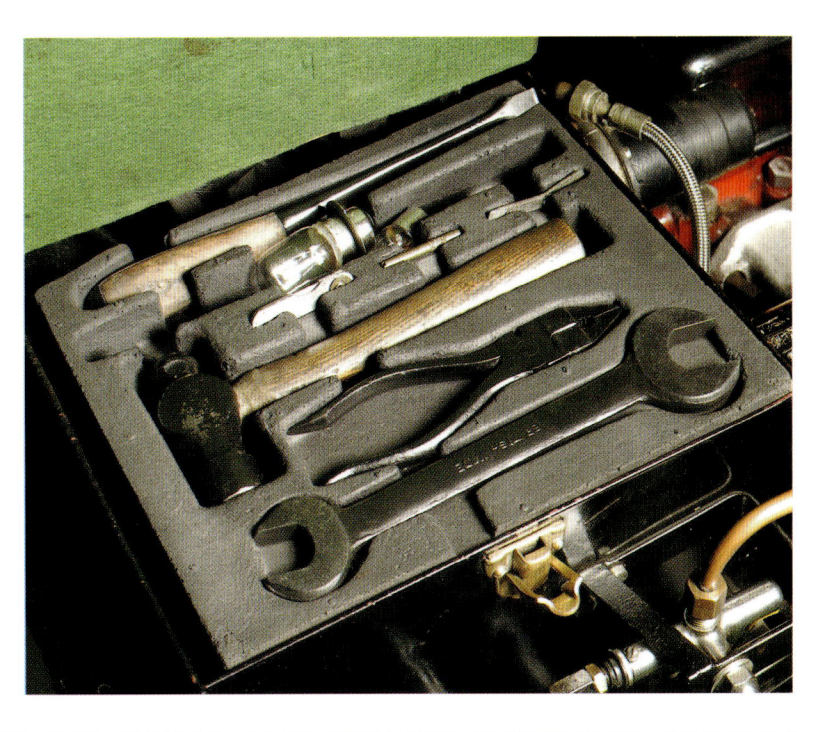

TA engine block showing its tappet chest. This engine belongs to Lech Zakrewski.

This type of sidelamp, Lucas 1130, was fitted to TAs, TBs and TCs.

be obtained. The only automatic device was the cut-out in the control box.

Instead of a dry clutch, the clutch in the TA was designed to run in oil, very like the early VA and following current Morris/Wolseley practice. The oil was supplied via a feed from the crankshaft. The clutch plate was fitted with 140 corks and engaged with a 652.2lb pressure plate with twelve springs in it.

The gearbox also came out of the Morris parts bin, and was modified internally quite early on in its production. Up to engine number MPJG 633 its ratios were: first 3.715:1, second 2.2:1, third 1.42:1, and reverse 4.78:1, top being direct. From MPJG 634 these changed so that first became 3.454:1, second to 2.04:1, third to 1.32:1 and reverse 4.44:1. It was operated by a remote gear change in an aluminium extension and had synchromesh on third and fourth gears only. This was, of course, a rather modern invention at that time. The 'box had an oil capacity of 2 pints of EP140 gear oil and is of a substantial construction. It never seems to wear out its gears. The only maintenance needed is replacement of bearings and forks.

The propshaft was a Hardy Spicer unit with universal joints fore and aft and a sliding splined front yoke at the gearbox end. The rear axle was new, derived from the Morris 10/4, with a 4.89:1 spiral bevel final drive. This gearing gave the car a road speed of 16.66mph per 1000rpm in top gear on 19-inch wheels fitted with 4.50 section tyres. At maximum power, 4800rpm, the car had a top speed of 80mph which in those days was substantial. A cruising speed of 65-70mph was possible, and these days more easily obtainable.

Like the gearbox, the final drive unit also uses EP140 oil. It doesn't smell very nice, and will often leak from a gearbox round the speedometer drive housing.

Replenishing the gearbox is easy, because it has a dipstick. Topping up the differential unit is again anti-social, as you have to remove a level plug and fill the diff until oil runs out. As it is a thick oil it takes its time to show, and then drips out for a long time. A drip tray is essential.

Originally the oil was retained in the rear axle and prevented from leaking into the rear brakes by a bearing oil seal in the hub, a paper gasket between the hub and the half-shaft hub, and a brass insert in the axle end with a reverse scroll on it. All these parts wear and oil gets all over the rear brakes. Nowadays, in addition to the conventional oil seal in the hub, you can buy the hub nut that bolts the inner hub to the axle with an integral oil seal. This completely halts the leakage of oil and means that the rear brakes take their full part in the braking department. It also has the peculiar side effect of drying out the rear wheel cylinders, so that if left unused they seize up, like front ones do from time to time.

The TA was the first MG Midget to utilise

A nice side shot of one of the first TAs, possibly JB 9446, which did service as a press car.

hydraulic braking. The Lockheed system was fitted, and the drums were of 9in diameter front and rear. Hydraulic brakes had only been introduced to the general motoring public a few years earlier, and the system was viewed with suspicion. Accordingly it was a bold leap of faith for the MG Car Company to introduce them, though there was some comfort to be had from their record, as the 2-litre SA saloon car had already had them for virtually two years before the TA was launched. Favourable road test reports helped their acceptance.

On the TA the brakes were of the single leading shoe type, with one wheel cylinder at the top of the backplate operating front and rear shoes. The system was operated from a master cylinder slung alongside the offside chassis member just inside it and just aft of the pedal fulcrums. It was actuated by a pushrod running down from the bottom of the brake pedal and swinging in a cup to give it a universal joint before entering the front of the master cylinder. The wheel cylinders at the front are considerably larger than the ones at the back, to provide a forward braking bias. Brake adjustment was by a couple of double-cam arrangements operated with a spanner on a large nut on the reverse of the brake back plate. The TA's are remarkably good brakes and, with only a change of linings, will safely retard a highly-tuned racing T-type that has a top speed of 115mph-plus to check. As this is between 40 and 50mph above the legal speed limit you can see that the road car has quite a lot of reserve in its braking system.

The handbrake is a frequent cause of upset in the annual safety inspection – the MoT test – that cars in Britain must submit to. This is because it is of the "fly off" type, which a lot of modern-day mechanics and motorists haven't

The fly-off handbrake and the flat-topped gear knob, which was unique to the pre-war cars.

The door tread plate on the TA.

On the TA engine 1¼in SU HV3 semi-downdraught carburettors were fitted.

encountered. Pressing the button in the top of the lever locks rather than releases the brake. To release it one simply pulls the lever towards one and then lets go, so that it "flies off". The lever operates a cross-shaft across the chassis, with lugs attached to each end into which the cable ends are slotted, with an adjustment bolt at the threaded end of each cable. The handbrake is adjustable by a wing nut at the bottom of the lever, by the cam adjuster on each brake, and by tensioning the cables with the locking nuts. Proper adjustment is achieved when the lugs face downwards directly at the floor and the lever then pulls back with an increasing and regular load. Both rear wheels will lock in a stationary position, and should do at moderate speed as well. Handbrake turns are then an easy adventure on gravel and loose surfaces!

The standard TA body is of the Ulster configuration, that is with the separate fuel tank bolted to the back of the body and not integral with it or slung underneath it between the chassis members, as in saloon cars of that era. The body is traditionally constructed of steel panels over ash formers. On each side of the car is a small all-steel subframe bolted to the chassis that holds the timbers for the door sills and provides the outline for the rear decking behind the passenger compartment, as well as the general line of the body. The scuttle/bulkhead is attached to an ash framework between the front of the doors that provides a strong and flexible mounting.

The running boards form a straight line with the front wings and rear wings when viewed directly either from the front or the back of the car. They are quite wide, with three longitudinal rubbing strips. The front wings had a pointed front but formed from a rounded curve so they had a softer appearance compared to the front wings on the TC, which came in several styles but with much sharper points at the front. On the early cars the rear wings were narrow and un-ribbed and dropped a long way over the back of the wheel. From 1938 the rear wings were wider, with a central rib down the rear half, and terminated slightly higher at the back than the originals.

The TA body is coded B270, and in 1936, 1937 and early 1938 its rear wings were very narrow and not unlike the PB's. The petrol tank was therefore wider, to fill the gap, and held 15 gallons. Later cars adopted the wider wings that found their way, with slight modifications, on to the TB and TC. Petrol tanks shrank to 13½ gallons. No petrol gauges were fitted to these cars and the TA and TB never even had a warning lamp. Instead they incorporated a petrol reserve tap, operated from the dashboard, attached to the reserve petrol line. Two pipes ran to this device, the first drawing petrol from the tank through a raised outlet about 2 gallons' depth from the bottom of the tank. This ran straight through to the petrol pump with the tap turned to "main". Once only two gallons remained the resulting splutter would remind the driver to turn the tap to "reserve". The two-way valve consisted of a cork. Over time this dried out and a lot of owners connected the reserve line directly to the fuel pump, so the main line was blocked off. Petrol reserves and

Here we have the metalwork that braces the body sides, with the main side timbers affixed showing the door openings.

The metal parts of the body, with the scuttle in the foreground, side panels, doors with their hinge brackets and striking plates, rear wheel arches and the rear bodywork covering.

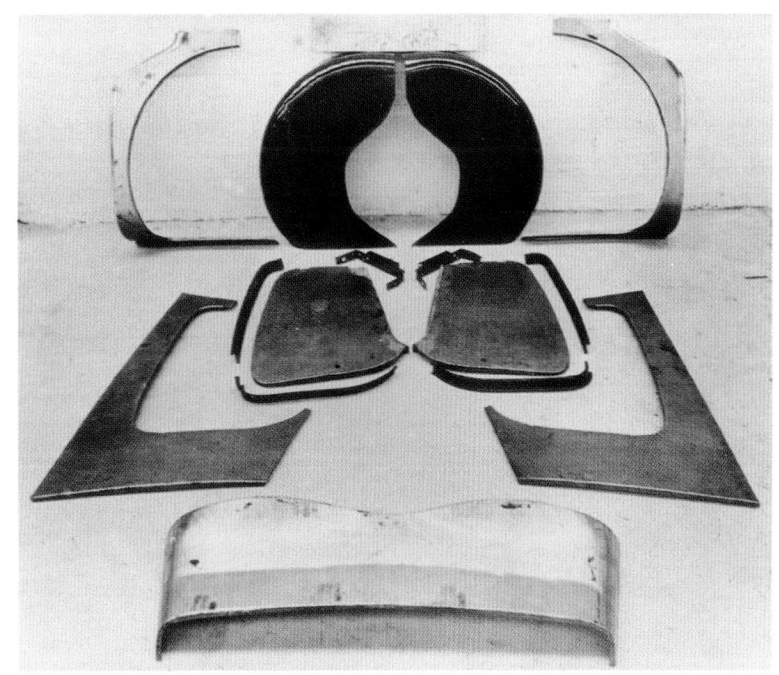

Far left: A bare body frame awaiting panels.

Left: The made up body, with trim, door locks and handles in place.

These are the two doors - their construction is very simple.

The dashboard construction, first the woodwork and then with the instruments fitted. These and the previous photographs are thought to be of the prototype TA.

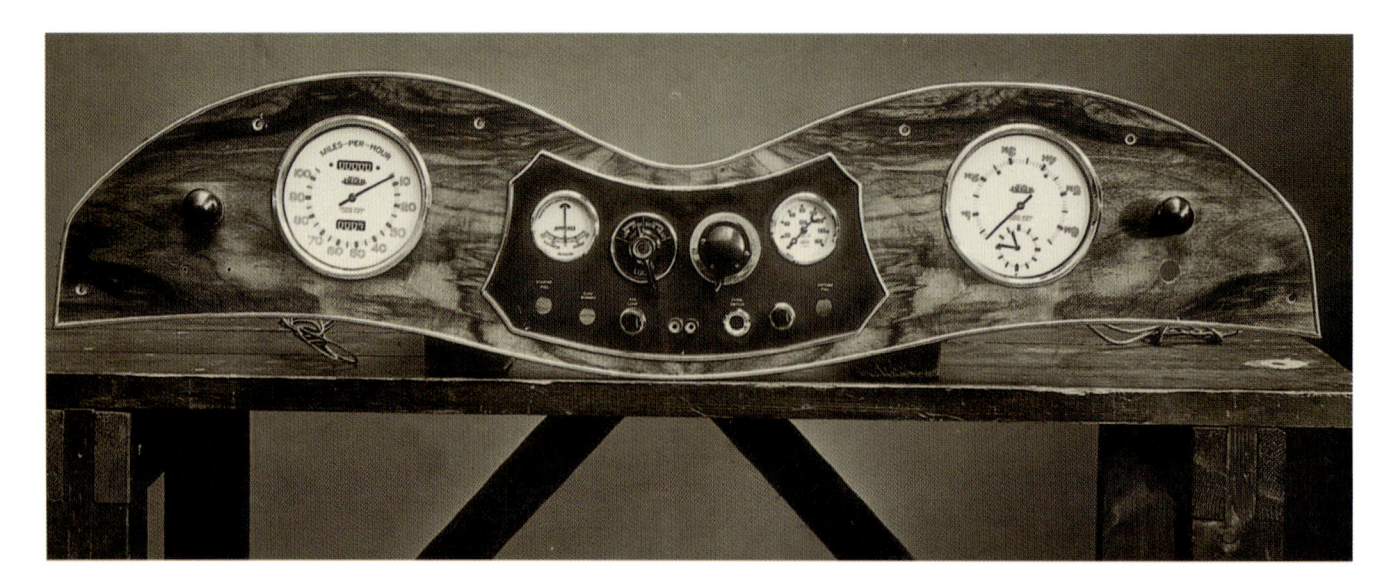

consumption are judged by a plethora of dipsticks that individual owners have made to suit their whims.

Apart from the sports two-seater, from 1938 onwards MG also offered a Tickford drophead coupé body. This was a much more civilised motor car, with a sumptuously trimmed interior. The doors remained front-opening but were higher, to shoulder level, and had winding glass windows. The three-position hood was of pram type with external hood irons and was lined. The car was a lot heavier than the two-seater and as a result rode and drove a bit differently, but it provides a civilised form of two-seater motoring. In addition two Airline coupés were produced, one of which still exists, I believe, in Canada.

The dashboard in the two-seater was double humped in front of the driver and passenger, and in front of the passenger was a Jaeger 5-inch speedometer with a white face and gold numbers and needle. It read from 0 to 100mph and was fitted with a total mileage recorder as well as a 1000-mile trip recorder.

In the centre of the dashboard was a metal panel, sprayed black, containing two 2-inch instruments, the ammeter on the left and the oil pressure gauge on the right. Between these is the combined ignition/lights/charging switch. The ignition was operated by a key, and the lights by a large black rotary switch in the order of side lamps, head lamps, low and high charge. Alongside this is the combined horn/dip switch. The horn push is a black bakelite item and behind it is a left/right dip switch for low and high beam.

Along the bottom of this panel were, from right to left, the slow running control, the turn switch for the panel lights, the ignition warning light and the inspection lamp socket (a red and black socket, also useful for a windscreen heater and, with a little bit of ingenuity, a mobile

As an early TA, Roger's car has the long, narrow rear wings, with no stiffening ribs, of this model. A full tonneau cover is fitted – the standard factory-supplied tonneau only covered the space behind the seats.

MG T SERIES IN DETAIL

The apron across the dumb irons has six transverse louvres. TAs would normally have radiator slats matching the interior trim colour, but there were exceptions.

The TA Tickford drophead coupe, of which more than 300 were made by Salmons & Sons on the TA and TB chassis. It had wide doors, wind-up windows, individual seats, extra wood trim and a fully-lined hood.

phone charger as well!). Next to this is another turn switch for the fog lamp. Lastly are the choke and starter pulls, sitting underneath the ammeter. In front of the driver is the Jaeger 5-inch chronometric rev counter, reading to 6000rpm. An electric clock sits in the bottom of this instrument, adjusted by a cable with a knurled knob on the end, similar to the one fitted to the speedometer to adjust the trip recorder. On each side of the central panel were map reading lights in the form of chromed twistable bulb shrouds with the bulb fitted in a black base. The light shone out of a hole cut into the chromed shroud.

The standard steering wheel had a black rim and three flat black blades running down to the hub, with an MG emblem on the boss. The wheel was attached to the column by a keyed shaft and locking bolt. A very popular after-market accessory is the Bluemels wheel, which has four sprung spokes. It usually came with a black rim, though a bone-coloured one was also available.

A wide choice of sports cars was produced in the 1930s Some, like the AC, Alvis and Aston Martin were vastly more expensive than the MG and thus, so to speak, out of its class. Others, for instance the Lea-Francis or the Riley, were not quite so exclusive but were still not within the price range of the potential MG buyer. The TA's main competitors during its production were perhaps the cars which most closely resembled it in looks, specification and price, and these were the models produced by BSA, Frazer Nash, HRG and Singer. Both Morgan and BSA produced three-wheeler cars at the time as well as four-wheelers.

BSA's two-seater Scout, introduced in 1935, was innovative in that it incorporated front-wheel drive. A pretty car, it had a four-cylinder sidevalve engine of 1203cc producing 28bhp at 4000rpm on a very low 5.8:1 compression ratio. Its 63.5mm bore was the same as the TA's, but the stroke, at 95mm, was shorter than the MG's 102mm. Track at the front was 4ft and at the rear 3ft 8in, and the wheelbase was 7ft 6in. There were 18-inch wire wheels running 4.50 section tyres, and a 6-volt electrical system. The gear lever emerged from the dashboard – thence the linkage ran to the very front of the car, as the

A pleasing and interesting shot, taken on a tour round Nova Scotia. The Tickford is almost as original with the exception of the lamps on the rear wings. The TD is fitted with a low-level luggage rack which makes the car much easier and safer to drive.

The very rare TA Airline Coupe. This is a larger version of the Coupe body fitted to a few P-types. It is thought only two TA Airline cars were made. This one was last heard of in Nova Scotia.

gearbox was ahead of the engine. Since the latter produced not much more than half of the TA's output, the Scout could not be a serious competitor in terms of performance, but its general appearance was similar and it possibly had the better handling of the two because of its independent front suspension. And the two-seater cost only £159.10s. Yet it was more of a touring car than a sports car: on its dash, for example, a clock took the place of a rev counter. The last versions of the Scout, produced in 1939, had 32bhp and a 70mph top speed. If the engine had been more amenable to tuning it might have been quite a competitive with the TA.

Frazer Nash cars had been built since the 1920s and were renowned for their sporting prowess. The 1½-litre Frazer Nash was a very popular sports car of the 1930s, being regarded as a real man's motor car and, with its chain transmission, demanding a special driving technique. Its design did not change substantially from the 1920s into the 1930s but the cars were less civilised than the TA, being renowned for their oiliness. The Frazer Nash was considerably more expensive than the MG – so perhaps it should not gain a mention here – but it epitomised the sports car of the era and had a wonderfully vintage look to it. The author recalls an old 'Nash which used to turn up on Saturday mornings in Llandiloes, mid-Wales, and park in the middle of the main road, where its very ancient occupants would emerge from it in voluminous coats, scarves and hats to do their weekly shop. This was during the late 1950s, when double yellow lines and traffic wardens had not been invented. I always thought its style beat my TA's, though that was also a rather dilapidated motor car!

A true alternative to the TA would be the 1½-litre HRG, priced at £395 though only made in tiny numbers. It is related to the Frazer Nash in that originally the GN car had been produced by Godfrey and Archie Frazer-Nash. Archie Frazer-Nash went on to produce the Frazer-Nash and Godfrey joined Messrs Hawford and

THE TA

This is a one-off. A very elegant Park Ward-bodied TA drophead that Hemmo de Groot brought over to Silverstone in 1992. It is a 1936 model and was converted in the 1940s. (Photo by Warren Marsh)

Dashboard of the TA, with the 5-inch Jaeger rev counter in front of the driver and the speedometer on the far side. The steering wheel with three flat spokes is the standard item.

MG T SERIES IN DETAIL

The BSA Scout – a possible alternative to the T-type MG but a lot slower.

The double humps of the scuttle are a traditional sports car feature, intended perhaps to give a little protection from the elements.

Robins to produce the HRG. This was a traditional-looking sports car fitted with a 1496cc Meadows overhead-valve power unit producing 58bhp at 4500rpm and giving 85mph. It was of a similar weight to the TA at 14cwt and came to be a serious competitor with T-types, especially on the racetracks after World War II. In 1939 the chain-driven overhead-camshaft Singer engine was adopted and the HRG became even more akin to the TA with a capacity of 1100cc and an output of 44bhp. It was capable of about 75mph but the engine could take a bit of tuning and some models could exceed 80mph.

During the 1930s the Morgan Car Company was primarily producing its famous range of three-wheeler cars but in 1935 introduced the four-wheeled 4/4 model, with looks similar to the MG's and initially fitted with a 1122cc Coventry Climax engine giving 78mph. It had independent front suspension by sliding pillars, a Morgan tradition, and the two-seater was priced at £194. It provided much the same type of raw, open-air motoring experience as the TA and was equally popular for competition use. This and later 4/4s offered during the T-types' production were very rugged, and early models have lasted just as well as early T-types. They were built on a relatively substantial chassis which benefited from an automatic undersealing process – the early cars had engines which were not particularly oil-tight and the oil chucked out from the engines, gearboxes and back axles helped to preserve the chassis through the casual times of the 1950s and 1960s, when pre-war sports cars could be bought for next to nothing and used and abused by students before the cars started to acquire a classic status in the 1970s.

The 100mph speedometer with the map reading lamp beside it.

However, the MG's greatest rival until 1937, when Singer pulled out of sports cars, was undoubtedly that company's Nine, which was powered by a very sweet 972cc ohc engine. Launched in 1933, the early models prompted the MG Car Company to uprate their PA into the PB as the Singer was stealing the honours from MGs in trials and rallies. The Nine had a lowered frame, a remote change for the four-speed gearbox, hydraulic brakes, twin carburettors and very attractive lines. Also offered was the Nine Le Mans, with high-lift camshaft, counterbalanced crankshaft and the ability to run up to 6000rpm, the equivalent of 75mph in top gear. At its launch price of £215 it offered stiff competition to the then-current MGs. Meanwhile, the apple of the Singer enthusiast's eye would have been the 1934-36 1½ Litre Le Mans, an ohc six-cylinder, triple-carburettor model with an 85mph maximum and excellent manners.

Unfortunately, during the 1935 TT a team of three Singer Nines dramatically crashed at the same spot, caused by breakage of their steering drop arms. Although this was not the fault of Singer - the drop arms having

A Singer tackling a loose surface on the Scottish Rally. These cars with their ohc engines - 972cc four-cylinder and 1493cc six-cylinder - were MG's greatest rivals in the mid-1930s.

Riley made some truly desirable sports cars in the 1930s. This is a 1935 MPH. A choice of three six-cylinder engines was available, from 1458cc to 1726cc, and any of the cars could reach 90mph, but at £550 it was more than double the price of a TA.

A Morgan and an HRG, both competitors to the T-types, at the petrol pump in Patterdale on the 1952 RAC Rally. The date is postwar, but both makes looked much the same in pre-war days.

been made by an outside supplier – the cars' reputation suffered.

The TA, produced at a price of £222, generally won on price, as other makes of sports cars were usually more expensive. This has always been a factor in MG's success: their ability to produce a good-looking, good-handling, well-equipped and civilised sports car that attracted both the sporting motorist and discerning drivers with no competitive ambition.

Production changes to the TA

It is a commonly held belief that after the TA was launched in 1936 the only real change to it was when it received the wider wings and the narrower petrol tank. In fact there was a continuous programme of improvement of components, as evidenced by a series of confidential, technical information sheets printed by the factory. These are as follows:

4/11 1936 Gearbox ratios changed at engine number MPJG684 and slightly closer ratios introduced.

4/11 1936 Piston design changed at engine number MPJG697.

4/11 1936 Rubber pads, part number S68/25, fitted to clutch and brake pedals from chassis number TA0717.

4/11 1936 Moulded rubber tool trays, part numbers S68/23RH and S68/24LH, supplied in place of tool roll, part number P330/100, after the first 250 cars. Wooden jack support block, part number S113/3, fitted in the tool box from chassis number TA0682.

4/11 1936 Rubber cover, part number S68/21, fitted over the gearbox in place of carpet, part number B269/168, from body number 507/4764.

5/11 1936 Silencer and rear exhaust pipe assembly, part number MG696/8, which has an auxiliary expansion chamber in the rear pipe, superseded at chassis number TA0616 by part number 696/5 in which this auxiliary expansion chamber is omitted.

27/2 1937 Commencing at body number 629/4870, a rubber draught excluder, part number S68/26 and retainer part number S.69/5, fitted around the base of the clutch and brake pedals.

27/2 1937 Commencing at chassis number TA1074, revised front shock absorbers fitted. These are interchangeable with the old type, but are of different internal construction and can be identified by the letters AR cast on the body instead of AC. It is very important that these new shock absorbers are fitted in pairs only, or uneven suspension will result.

30/4 1937 Improved type of swivel pin oil seal incorporated, commencing at chassis number TA1253.

In place of the sealing disc, a felt washer and retainer are fitted, secured by a bolt in the top of the swivel pin.

30/4 1937 Stronger steering arms fitted. These are in Vibraq steel and the portion which is secured to the steering knuckles is of even section instead of being stepped. This entails the fitting of larger bolts. Only the latest type levers will be supplied as replacements. This change commenced at chassis number TA1255.

30/4 1937 In order to bring the nut securing the offside engine tie strap bracket into a more accessible position, the hole in the engine front bearer plate was moved ½in towards the centre. This, however, resulted in the misalignment of the offside tie strap. A modification has now been introduced to the chassis frame's second cross tube, consisting of a double bracket, which will suit either position. The new bracket commenced at chassis number TA1657 and was also fitted to chassis number 1632-1647 inclusive.

1/5 1937 Double-row front thrust bearing for the rear axle bevel pinion fitted in place of single-row thrust bearing, commencing at chassis number TA1254. It should be noted that the latest type of crown wheel and pinion is suitable for use with either thrust bearing, since the only difference is a longer bearing surface.

1/5 1937 Improved valve springs fitted. The new springs are of ground wire and have 8 effective coils (inner) and 6.3 (outer) instead of 6.5 and 5 respectively. Only the latest type of valve springs will be supplied as replacements. The new springs commenced at engine number MPJG1245.

25/6 1937 Commencing at engine number MPJG1637, new type push rods fitted. These are of an improved material specification but are interchangeable with the original type. Only the latest type of push rods will be supplied for replacements.

25/6 1937 Commencing at engine number MPJG1605, triple valve springs fitted.

28/6 1937 Commencing at engine number MPJG1514, modified type of oil filter fitted. The oil is now fed from the oil filter casting direct to the oil gallery in the cylinder block, instead of through an external oil pipe.

28/6 1937 Commencing at chassis number TA1306, return spring for the handbrake fitted. The spring is secured to the cross shaft by means of a clip and anchored to the offside tunnel support bracket.

28/6 1937 Petrol tank, part number MG731, replaces MG685, when the narrower body is fitted.

28/6 1937 Modified type of body fitted at the rear, necessitating a narrower petrol tank and new rear wings. This new body can be identified by type number B270 stamped on the body number plate secured to the nearside body pillar under the scuttle, the type number of the original body being B269. In addition the seat squab on these new bodies is hinged to the seat slides instead of having separate peg and rack adjustment.

28/6 1937 Further to the previous technical information sheet, rear wings, part numbers S80/13O/S, and S80/14N/S replaced part numbers S80/7O/S, and S8/60/8NS, when the narrower body is fitted.

5/1 1938 New road wheels fitted, with the spokes secured to the well of the rim instead of the side of the rim. This increases the offset of the wheel, thereby widening the track by approximately $5/16$in. This commenced from chassis number TA1770.

17/2 1938 Slow running return spring now fitted which is hooked at one end to the carburettor slow running lever pin, in place of the split pin, and at the other through a hole drilled in the air intake pipe strap. The above commenced at chassis number TA1990.

17/2 1938 Improved type of jet control introduced, in which a stop bracket is secured between the rear carburettor and the induction manifold, and the extended jet link on the rear carburettor, previously acting as a stop for the outer casing of the jet control wire, is replaced by the short link as fitted to the front carburettor. The fitting of the stop bracket necessitates the use of a packing piece between the front carburettor and the induction manifold and two extra carburettor joints. This modification commenced at chassis number TA1926. In addition the jet level connecting rod is now fitted with fork ends instead of ball joints, necessitating new jet operating levers with $3/16$in diameter holes for the fork ends instead of $1/4$in diameter holes for the ball joints. This modification commenced at chassis number TA1877. A new solid "ball and lever" throttle spindle coupling also replaces the flexible type, commencing at chassis number TA1877.

11/4 1938 A few isolated cases of wear taking place of the wheel bearings have been brought to our notice. This wear has been brought about by clearance between the outer ring of the race and the shoulder of the housing. This complaint, which is of rare occurrence, maybe rectified by the insertion of a shim.. Part in question being MG689/143 Shim for rear hub ball race.

11/4 1938 Commencing at axle No 2570, new bevel pinion housing. This new housing has its bore stepped to relieve the forward outer journal from radial loads. The part in question being as follows: MG689/144 Bevel Pinion Housing, replaces MG689/134.

11/4 1938 Commencing at chassis number TA2249, a new propeller shaft having larger diameter journal pins and smaller needle bearings fitted. The new propeller shaft is strictly interchangeable with the old type and only the latest one will be supplied for service replacements. Details are as follows: A1070 propeller shaft 2½in diameter x 43 $13/16$in long, replaces A842.

11/4 1938 Commencing at engine number MPJG2430, a new crankshaft, having two oilways drilled diametrically opposite in the main bearing journals, replaces the present type with one oil hole. In addition, commencing at engine number MPJG2532, new crankshaft main bearings having the oil grooves offset have been fitted.

11/4 1938 Commencing at chassis number TA2253, Tecalemit grouped nipple lubrication system fitted. This necessitates the drilling of several holes in the chassis frame side members and dash for pipe clips, and welding of two brackets for the Tecalemit identification plates to the dash.

11/4 1938 Improved type of oil gauge pipe, which prevents the possibility of fracture due to engine movement. The new arrangement consists of a flexible pipe and a copper pipe, joined together by means of a brass connector, which is secured to a bracket welded to the nearside chassis frame side member, in a position 22$^{13}/_{16}$in rearwards of the front axle centre line.

11/4 1938 Commencing at chassis number TA2254, stiffer front springs fitted The new springs have seven main leaves instead of five main leaves and two rebound leaves, and also the latest type of leaf clips. New front shock absorber brackets and spring securing bolts are also necessary.

6/5 1938 Commencing at engine number MPJG2622, oil deflecting plate fitted for the camshaft sprocket, part number MG706/437.

13/2 1939 Commencing from the first Tickford Coupé model and on the two-seater model from chassis number TA2882, telescopic adjustable steering wheel fitted with new steering gear to suit. This new gear has a ratio of 11:1 instead of 8:1 as formerly.

13/2 1939 Commencing at chassis number TA 2518, new type greaser nipples fitted to suit a new hydraulic grease gun.

25/5 1939 New rear number plate, part number S112/6, fitted in place of part number 1124 to accommodate a new stop and tail lamp. For service purposes part number S112/8 as fitted to the Series TB Midget will replace part number S112/6.

25/5 1939 Commencing at body number B269/10554, new D-shaped stop and tail lamp fitted, to improve the illumination of the rear number plate. This necessitates the fitting of a new number plate.

Accessories

In January 1937 the MG Car Company issued a list of approved extra equipment for the TA. This list is as follows:

Aero screens
Bonnet strap and fittings
Spare bulb carrier
Cigar lighter
Paint to a colour of choice, excluding metallic finish
Double dimming headlamps
Fire extinguisher
Different coloured hoods
Horn and dipper switch arm on the steering column instead of on the dash
Inspection lamp
Built in jacks, front and rear
Luggage carrier
Battery master switch
Reversing lamp
Second spare wheel
Speedometer reading in kilometres
A spot lamp, with a special bracket
Alternative steering whcels, an Ashby one and a Bluemels one, categorised as "Malcolm Campbell"
Stoneguards for the headlamps
Stop and tail lamp on the nearside instead of the offside
An oil temperature gauge
A water temperature gauge
A full tonneau cover
Trafficators

It was also possible to have the upholstery a special colour and the wheels painted to choice. The dimming headlamps and the kilometre speedometer were fitted exclusively to export models going into Europe.

The TA Press Cars

The MG Car Company was always good at publicising itself, right from the start, and when the TA was announced Cecil Kimber was quick off the mark in making cars available for long-term testing. One of these, JB 9446, was entrusted to the well-known photographer W J Brunell, who took it on a tour through France, Belgium, Holland and into Germany in 1936, during the rise of Nazism. The photos that follow where taken on this trip, which was recorded at the time in the motoring journals.

Brunell and JB 9446 were accompanied by another TA, two P-types and the Lagonda that are featured in these photographs. There were also two other P-types and a Riley in the group, and other drivers included S Ison, W G Dutton, G R K Richards, W G Allen, K S Haywood and Miss W Sloan.

JB 9446 car was one of a three TAs, JB 9444 to 9446, that were registered by the factory for various purposes. 9445, chassis TA 0267, was used as a trials car by Godfrey "Goff" Imhoff in 1937 as reserve for the factory-sponsored Cream Cracker and Musketeer teams. In 1938 it was acquired by George Murray Frame, who ran it in the Highlanders team that year. In 1964 it was owned by D A Cook in Oxford, but has not been seen since. 9444, chassis TA 0298, is still around and has been owned by Angus Peacock for very many years. 9446 is owned by Jill Partridge, I believe. In their day all three were also used as press cars and loaned to motoring magazines.

A scene wonderfully evocative of the era, taken in the town of Arras in northern France. The TA is in the foreground - note the cooling flaps in the lower scuttle panel.

There was also a PB, here with its bonnet up outside the party's hotel in St Quentin, where the staff turned out to see the cars. The chefs, we are told, prepared some excellent meals.

Still in France, and drawing another small crowd keen to ask about the cars and get their picture taken.

Evening shadows beside a canal in Bruges, Belgium.

The party included this Lagonda and MG PA, seen here outside an inn in the Dutch village of Molen Eind.

A German family return from the fields past the travel-stained MG.

JB 9446 car also took part in the International Alpine Trial. Here we see the lower stage of the Furka Pass.

A pause while ascending the Brunig pass on the way to Meiringen in the International Alpine Trial.

TA Driving Impressions

I was privileged to drive the Cream Cracker Trials car originally used by "Jesus" Jones as a works car in trials before the war. This particular example, registered ABL 964, is now owned by Ken Selby and is tucked away in a corner of south west Wales. It has participated in modern-day classic trials including the Lands End, the Exeter and the Edinburgh, as well as more local club events. For 18 months before I drove it the car had been laid up, but Ken drove it 50-odd miles up the Welsh coastline before heading inland over Plynlimon to our meeting point.

The car has a normal 1292cc engine with a very slightly raised compression ratio. The only additional aid to tuning is a "tweaked" camshaft. Other modifications made to these works cars included the fitting of larger Luvax shock absorbers and a brake master cylinder derived from the MG WA Saloon. This is a twin master cylinder with a fail-safe arrangement of brake pipes.

The dashboard is standard except for a water temperature gauge on the right and an oil temperature gauge on the left. On this chilly day the needles stayed fairly close to zero! The rev counter is red lined at 4800rpm and the main instruments, oil pressure gauge and ammeter have green faces.

Under the bonnet are twin one-inch SU carburettors with a standard air cleaner and the standard three-branch exhaust manifold. Both front and rear wings have been converted to the cycle type and there are no running boards. The headlamps have been converted to double-dipping – still using the old mechanical system so that there is a satisfactory clunk when the lamps are switched from main beam to dipped and vice versa. There was adequate room in the pedal arrangements for me to drive the car in desert boots. The accelerator was high in relation to the brake pedal but not in such a disabling way as in the TD I drove. We are reminded of the history of Ken's car by the Cream Cracker insignia on the bonnet, by the twin spare wheels behind the petrol tank and by a plate for displaying competition numbers at the left rear.

This TA's steering box has been modified with one of the Tompkins kits, which have been popular since the 1950s. The modification consists of an aluminium structure that sits on the steering box and has an adjustable peg connecting with the top of the sector shaft. The theory is that finer adjustment can be effected with this arrangement than with the original shim design, so that an exact amount of play can be dialled into the steering box setting. Recently, however, it has been reported that TAs, TBs and TCs fitted with this gear are suffering breakage of the sector shaft at the junction of the horizontal piece carrying the peg that meshes with the worm. Perhaps we shouldn't be surprised by this, as the single point of contact for adjustment is concentrated at the top of the sector shaft so that there is a bending strain on the horizontal piece

The "Jesus" Jones Cream Cracker team car, now owned by Ken Selby. It has been converted to cycle wings and there are no running boards.

which eventually causes it to fracture, with potentially serious consequences. The old-fashioned method of adjustment by means of shims spread the load-bearing area against the whole of the top plate (frequently described as a side plate as the normal position of these steering boxes was 90 degrees to that on the T-types). Over the years some people have crudely adapted the Tompkins principle, often by means of a screwed thread running through a captive nut in the top plate on to the top of the sector shaft. In view of the recent failures this is not to be recommended unless you include frequent crack testing of the steering internals as a routine maintenance operation, perhaps every 1000 miles.

On Ken's car there was quite an alarming amount of play in the steering, although the steering itself was smooth and easy. I also discovered fairly quickly that the brakes were not quite as good as they should be, probably due to seizure of one or two of the wheel cylinders during the car's lay up. Acceleration was brisk, but changing gear was complicated by the lack of synchromesh. Upward changes were relatively easy but it was necessary to double-declutch and match the revs when changing down. The crunching of gears soon lessened.

I drove the TA down the single-track road from my brother's house to the A470, the main road that links North and South Wales. On the bumpy single-track road it was not possible to drive at much more than 20-25mph due to the fact that the steering was slightly erratic, but once on the smooth surface of the A470 the car felt much easier and was capable of cruising at 55-60mph, provided that adequate allowance was made for winding on the steering before corners and leaving a good braking distance. Fortunately the roads were very light in traffic as we joined the A44 that goes down to Rhayader alongside the River Wye, running gently downhill through some fairly wide, fast corners which the TA took with ease.

We descended to the river junction of the Marteg and the Wye and turned on to another single-track road up the Marteg valley. This road twists and dives and I found the brakes were starting to warm up and become much more responsive. I had also got used to the steering, so was able to pilot the car through these corners and dips with a quiet confidence, accompanied by a lovely growl from the exhaust. There was even time to observe a red kite flying low down in the valley and admire its reddish-brown back and wings.

Once behind the TA engine you quickly come to appreciate the amount of torque it delivers and the fact that it can remain in the higher gears at very low revs in much the same way as a supercharged XPAG engine would behave. This characteristic brought home to me how suitable this engine is for trialling, why before the war the Cream Cracker and Musketeer teams would frequently take a clean sweep in the results, and why, after nearly 70 years, TAs can still take to the hills and reap their just rewards. It was only the ultimate weakness of the MPJG engine, with its unbalanced crankshaft and white metal bearings incurring large repair bills both in the factory and in dealers' workshops that made the adoption of the XPAG engine in the TB and successive cars inevitable. As for the rest of the TA, its robustness was quickly proved and the basic design, with improvements to cockpit space, remained in production until 1950, vestiges of it surviving in the TD and TF. The TA was a worthy progenitor of this whole range of cars, which caught the public's imagination in the 1930s and still continues to do so when seen on the road today. A joyous encounter on our trip in the TA was with a TC driven by a young man with his wife as passenger and their very young child between them. Who says these cars are for old fogies!

As a trials car it carries twin spares and a plate for displaying its competition number.

Chapter Three

The TB

In the late 1930s, Claude Baily, who was one of the Morris engineers at Cowley, turned to designing a successor to the Morris 10/4 engine that had found its way into the TA. The product of his labours was the Morris 10 engine of 1140cc known as the XPJM, and it was designed for use in the new 10hp M-Series Morris saloon. It came with a 63mm bore and a 90mm stroke – some 12mm shorter than the TA's – and could be described, in the context of those days, as a short-stroke engine. With a very modest 6.6:1 compression ratio it produced 37bhp at 4600rpm.

This unit then found its way into the Wolseley 10 in 1939 as an XPJW. The camshaft was of a 5; 45; 45; 5 timing, very symmetrical, and operated with a 0.019in valve rocker gap. The engine was a success from the start and MG immediately saw its potential. As the XPAG, it was bored out to 1250cc, the bore being enlarged to 66.5mm, and it ran with an average 7.25:1 compression ratio. A sportier camshaft with timings of 11; 57; 52; 24 was fitted. (The original Morris/Wolseley camshaft is not the same as the camshaft that was fitted to the later TDs and the TF, though it does have the same timing). The cylinder head was given larger valves and in this form produced 55bhp at 5200rpm. You will immediately see that it revved considerably more freely than the TA unit. Maximum torque was 64lb ft at 2600rpm. As the XPAG engine was somewhat larger and more robust than the Morris version, it had stronger connecting rods than the 1140cc unit and its crankshaft was made of a higher-quality cast iron.

During the winter of 1938/39 the engine was quietly dropped into a TA and from April 1939 the TB was born. This car wasn't publicly announced until July 1939, and of course production ceased soon after the outbreak of the Second World War in September of that year, so it had a very short life. Chassis numbers started at TB 0251 and finished 379 cars later at TB 0630.

This early XPAG engine differed from later versions and as will be seen from the appendices the engine was developed and subtly modified throughout its production, which went on, in the Wolseley form, as an XPAW engine until 1956. In the TB it was not fitted with a timing-chain tensioner and the side plate covering the tappet chest was of convex section

Another scene from the same shoot as the photo opposite, this one was used in the TB sales brochure although the picnic seems to be a rather glum affair. The Tickford's hood is in the sedanca position.

and tended to cut into the cork gasket, leading on some occasions to an enormous oil leak. This was because all the oil from the valve gear drained from the cylinder head down the inside of the tappet cover. Besides this possibility, the XPAG is known for not being completely oil tight. The rocker cover gasket is prone to slip if not held down squarely. If it does this on the offside you know about it soon enough, as smoke soon appears from the oil being burnt on the exhaust manifold. A leak on the other side is often more disastrous, as you don't detect this until the oil pressure disappears and the bearings start to rattle. When you get out to look the nearside of the engine, the chassis and body are covered in oil. These leaks can be prevented but the other one that is not so easy to sort out is from the rear main bearing. The seal is a scroll on the crankshaft and a thrower that is supposed to divert oil back into the sump. As the bearings wear this arrangement becomes less effective, so a little blob of oil dripped from a new engine can develop into quite a lake as time goes by.

The XPAG crankcase was considerably shorter in depth than that of the TA and finished $\frac{1}{8}$in below the centreline of the crankshaft. As in most four-cylinder engines the side thrust is

This photo was taken just before World War II and is of a TB Tickford. The chap leaning on the door is George Tuck, MG's Publicity Manager and the young lady is his wife. He had a long career in the motor industry, ending his days in South Africa.

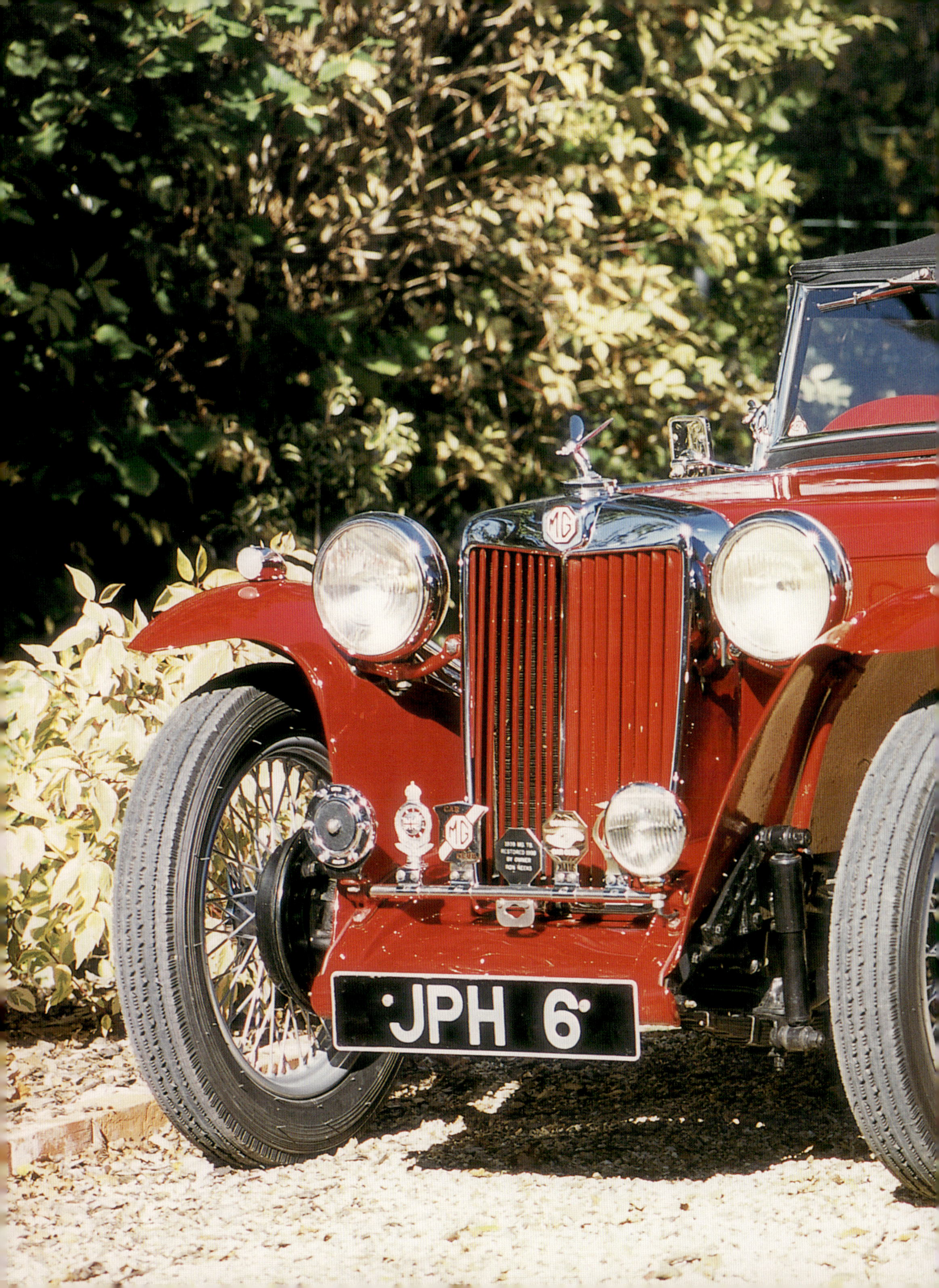
JPH 6

Ron Reeks' MG TB with hood up, sidescreens attached and a luggage rack. Note that the wheel spokes are now centre-laced.

MG T SERIES IN DETAIL

On the TB the petrol tank was narrower than on the TA and the rear wings wider. Just visible below the right wing is one of the copper pipes of the chassis lubrication system found on later TAs and all TBs. It is fed from two sets of grouped nipples.

taken by the centre main bearing and, once fitted with its aluminium finned sump, timing cover and aluminium bell housing, the XPAG unit has great rigidity. It was sufficiently robust to form the basis for an engine that could be tuned to produce, at its extreme, over 250bhp supercharged, as in the MG record breaker driven by Stirling Moss. Nowadays those who race T-types can develop the engine to reliably produce 140bhp.

Because the crankcase finished where it did the main bearings were split in the same way as the big ends are. Both main and big end bearings were now of the replaceable steel-backed

Ron Reeks's TB is chassis number TB 0623. The car was built in 1939 but not actually registered until September 1940, more than a year into the Second World War. A "Midge" mascot adorns its radiator.

52

thin-wall shell type, and are interchangeable with the shells in the Wolseley and Morris versions. In the TA's engine they were much deeper into the block, and were white metalled directly, so that they had to be line bored. The XPAG was a much more modern engine, forerunner of all the ohv pushrod engines offered by BMC, Ford and the Rootes Group. It had a considerable influence on engine design, and it survives in huge numbers. This and the fact that it is not particularly oil-tight has been the main reason why the T-type cars have survived so well. The engine is robust and its oil leaks stopped the chassis rusting. We all owe Mr Baily a huge debt of thanks.

The XPAG was rated for RAC rating purposes at 10.97hp. Its pistons are Aerolite solid skirt with a clearance of 0.002-.003in and are fitted

In this view the wider rear wings of the TB, with the central rib, are clearly shown.

The Reeks TB has a handsome set of custom-built luggage.

with two compression rings and one oil control ring. The pistons are clamped to the connecting rods at the gudgeon pins and the rods are 178mm long. The main bearings are 52mm in diameter and the big ends 45mm. The camshaft lies in the left hand side of the block, is driven by a chain from the crankshaft, and runs in three bearings, the centre one being split for ease of dismantling and re assembly. The cylinder head is a six-port design rather than the five-port head of the TA, so there are two separate exhaust ports in the middle of the head. The valve throat diameters are 25mm exhaust and 30mm inlet, with a valve seat angle of 30 degrees. The valves have double valve springs with a shut pressure of 93lb and an open pressure of 123lb. The valve lift is 8mm, the tappet clearance 0.019in.

A gear-type oil pump is driven off the front gear of the camshaft and is mounted externally

THE TB

The XPAG engine and gearbox as fitted to the TB. This could be termed the Mark 1 XPAG, as it had no timing chain tensioner and differently designed side and front covers. If this was the Mk.1, then the engine in the TC and early TD would be Mk 2, the late TD and 1250 TF XPAG engine would be Mk 3, and the one in the Mk II TD would be Mk 2½.

on the nearside of the block. The distributor is driven from the rear gear of the camshaft and sits on the left hand side of the cylinder block, above and to the right of the oil pump. It is held by a vernier clamp and a set bolt slotted into a groove in the distributor shaft housing to enable the distributor to be turned for timing. The early XPAG engines ran with a 70psi oil pressure and the minimum allowable was 40psi.

The carburettors are twin 1¼in SUs, again semi-downdraft as on the TA, mounted on a cast iron manifold. The standard carburettor needle is the ES, a weaker one was specified as the AP and a richer one as the EM. The fuel system is exactly the same as on the TA with twin fuel lines and the petrol reserve tap.

The water pump is now mounted on the front of the cylinder block instead of the head, giving a much shorter, more triangulated run to the belt that drives the pump and the dynamo. One of the XPAG engine's strengths is in the cooling system. It is arranged so that the water pump creates a circulation by delivering water under pressure to the back of the block. It does not actually go through the cylinder bores at all but is carried in an external water gallery on the

One of the first XPAG engines, in the prototype TB. Here you can see clearly the twin fuel lines and petrol reserve tap. The choke cable has not yet been fitted to the stabilising plate attached to the rear carburettor.

A nearside view of the same car and engine. The rev counter drive cable is yet to be attached to the back of the dynamo. You can see the Vernier adjustment for the distributor and the early oil filter.

55

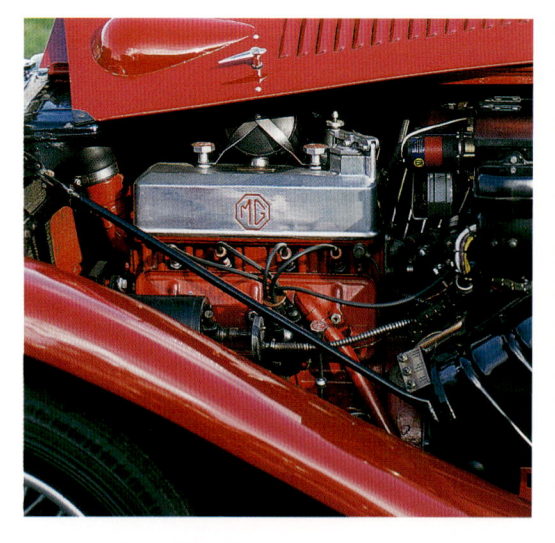

MG T SERIES IN DETAIL

Nearside view of the XPAG engine in the TB. This car has the cast aluminium rocker cover that could be specified.

On the side of the scuttle in this view of another TB can be seen the two fuel lines and the petrol reserve tap operated from the dashboard.

The TB gained a new air inlet manifold with the air cleaner at an angle over the rocker cover. The carburettors were now of the H2 type.

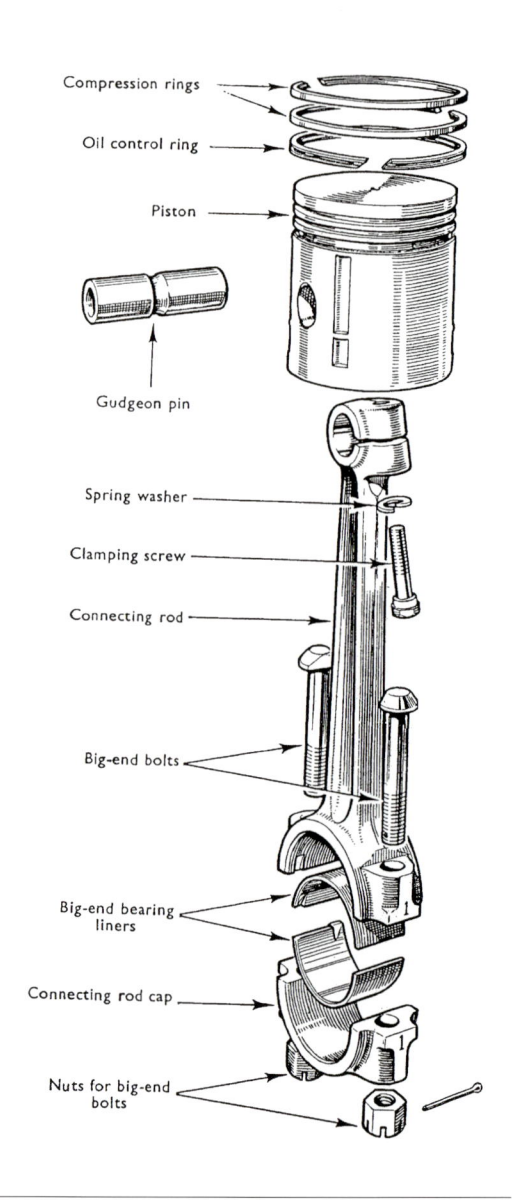

Piston and connecting rod assembly of the XPAG engine from TB to TF.

offside of the engine, so that the water rushes through there, up into the cylinder head, then back through the head and up via the thermostat into the radiator. The water in the block is virtually static and relies on what could be termed the old-fashioned thermosyphon priciple in that it moves gradually upwards to join the water in the head. This has the advantage of keeping a constant water temperature throughout the whole block and head, avoiding distortion and burnt valves.

Owners servicing these cylinder blocks have often discovered little holes bored through the jacket behind the core plugs in the gallery. These holes are not for cooling but are residues of the casting process and were drilled in the

56

blocks to enable the casting sand and machining swarf to be blasted out of the blocks. Should you find that your engine blocks possesses these holes, do not be tempted to drill them out to clear them as you will more than likely send the drill through into the cylinder bore. Instead, clean them out with wire and you will then find that it is a lot easier to flush the block and disperse the sludge inside which is often the cause of overheating.

The TB had a dry clutch of 7¼in diameter. The new gearbox was designed for the XPAG engine and differed from the TA 'box but was just as robust. It had a first gear ratio of 3.38:1, second 1.95:1, third 1.36:1 and a direct top. Reverse was also 3.38:1. The gearbox was slightly improved in that it had synchromesh on second as well as third and top gears, in other words a gear's advantage on the TA, and it had a nice remote change mechanism. The alloy remote change housing detached from the top of the gearbox, allowing you to inspect it easily. Very occasionally the little set bolts holding the forks would undo slightly, despite being wired, leading to jumping out of gear, especially if coming off the throttle suddenly into a corner in third gear. The only thing to watch when doing this is to make sure the springs that keep the shafts tight don't fall out of their holes, which are not particularly deep.

In view of the XPAG engine's willingness to rev, the rear axle ratio was lowered from 4.89:1

Plain, unsullied rear wings mark this out as a new TB undergoing a road test. The only rear lighting is the D-lamp. Once these cars had been around into the 1960s rear lights and reflectors often found their way on to the rear wings.

The radiator slats on this TB are correctly painted red to match the body and interior colour.

Close-up of the rear quarter of a TB. A nice chunky Dunlop 90 tyre and 19-inch wheel dominate.

to 5.125:1, the ratio between the pinion and the crown wheel being 8/41 instead of 8/39. This meant that for every 1000rpm the car would be doing 15.64mph in top gear. In the engine's standard form 5200rpm was the limit, and if one regularly explored revs above that level, particularly to 5800rpm, a torsional vibration would eventually break the front web of the crankshaft. Accordingly at 5200rpm a standard TB would have a top speed of approximately 81mph.

The final drive unit was offered with two alternatives to the standard 8/41 ratio. There was a lower ratio of 8/43 which was obviously designed to satisfy those who liked to trial the car, and a higher 8/39 for those who wanted a more comfortable cruising speed and a 5 per cent higher top speed. In a later chapter tuning will be discussed, and the relevance of these axle ratios will then become apparent.

Because the XPAG engine had its starter in a different position from that on the TA, the steering gear had to be moved higher up the front dumb iron of the chassis to give sufficient clearance. To a degree this altered the ratio of the drop arm to the drag link, and on the TB had a minor effect on the Ackerman angle that fortunately did not materially effect the car's handling qualities.

The suspension, although overtly identical with the TA's, differed very slightly in that it incorporated the uprated springs mentioned in the TA chapter as being introduced late in the production of that vehicle. As a result, although it is very hard to discern, the suspension on the very last of the TAs and the TBs was slightly softer. You would need a degree in cushion engineering to detect that! Otherwise the suspension was the same as the TA's and the handling was as good as, if not better than, the previous model's.

The TB was fitted with the same electrical system as the TA, ie a three-brush dynamo and the same arrangement of cut-out and fusebox, and the same two-position charging switch on the dashboard. On the back of the dynamo is a connection that enables the rev counter cable to be attached, with its reduction box. This can cause a mystery ignition fault to the unwary as, if it becomes loose, the reduction gearbox can

A lovely image of a TB all decked out for wartime motoring. This is an MG press photo engineered by George Tuck. His wife Sue and Mrs Propert are in the car, with the scene-stealing Siamese cat on the bonnet.

Tonneau cover and sidescreens in position. The door mirror is the factory item.

The headlamps have convex glasses with a U-shaped pattern.

The Lucas windscreen wiper motor was mounted at the top of the windscreen in front of the passenger's head. Today's health and safety police would not like it one bit.

swivel downwards so that it shorts against the low-tension terminal on the distributor. The engine will then go out. As on the TA, there were two six-volt batteries slung each side of the prop shaft in front of the back axle.

The body was the same as on the later TAs and two styles were offered: the two-seater sports car and the two-seater Tickford Coupé as it had appeared on the TA.

The car retained the Lockheed hydraulic braking system. The steering wheel was of the same type, a 17in Bluemels three-spoke, but the way that it was attached to the steering column differed in that it was splined on to the end of the shaft, rather than clamped as on all but the very latest TAs, and the boss was tightened on the spline by a pinch bolt. This change occurred late in the production of the TA. It meant that the steering wheel was adjustable in a fore and aft direction, which made it slightly easier to adjust to different drivers. On the TB, the dashboard and instrumentation remained the same as on the TA, although the instruments were more likely than not to be of the green-faced Jaeger type, which had also appeared on TAs along with the gold- and white-faced instruments that TAs also had.

Due to the onset of the war, only 379 cars were produced from chassis number TB0252 to TB0631. The first XPAG engine to be introduced into the TB would have been XPAG501 and in theory the last one fitted would have been XPAG 880. In fact it was probably 882, as the TC first came out with XPAG 883, which was fitted with a timing chain tensioner and a concave tappet cover plate.

The TB, with its XPAG engine, was soon

attracting those who liked to tune engines to produce more power and build special bodies for them. One such was the Monaco MG which had a very much lighter and narrower cycle-winged body and the engine enlarged to 1385cc. This was a very daring manoeuvre in those early days, as the XPAG block does not really take kindly to being bored out much beyond 60 thou, which was the factory-recommended overbore. Thus it was discovered quite early on that the engines could be enlarged, taking the bore from 66.5mm to 70mm, although it is possible that P R Monkhouse, who was behind the Monaco, bored out the engine and then lined it back to 1385cc. That was probably the case in view of the fact that they were promising to produce cars with either a 1250cc or a 1400cc engine. In these days taking the bore out to 70mm is quite common and reliable, although the cognoscenti use the XPAW block from the Wolseley 4/44, this being the strongest of all the XPA series of engine blocks, being produced in the mid-1950s.

As the TB was only produced between April and September 1939 there was very little opportunity for the cars to be actively developed in competition and they were never incorporated within the "Cream Cracker" or "Three Musketeer" trials teams. There is also no record of the TB being raced in that short period.

Of the 379 cars manufactured up to September many of them were not in fact sold until much later. The writer's TB was a case in point, not having been registered until the 19 July 1940, during the Battle of Britain, in Norfolk. Many of the cars were brought by servicemen, probably the wealthier pilots and higher ranks buying the TB new, with the more impecunious officers and in some cases the non-commissioned having second-hand TAs or possibly M-types, P-types and J-types. Douglas Bader is believed to have owned one as did Guy Gibson, the commander of the Dam Busters raid. Even the designer of the "bouncing bomb" which the Dam Busters used, Barnes Wallis, is reputed to have owned a TA.

At this stage it might be worth mentioning, the TB being the last of the post-vintage MGs built before the war, that there existed then and still exists now - in certain circles - a snobbery towards MG owners. After all, the MG was a cheap and cheerful sports car using mass-

The red TB has modern non-standard telescopic shock absorbers; the original lever-arm shock absorbers are seen in the accompanying picture (below) of the front suspension of another TB.

Lucas supplied the central instrument panel. The switches were clearly labelled. The device to the right of the ignition/lights switch is the combined horn push/dip switch.

The rev counter read to 6000rpm and had a clock set into it it.

produced parts from the Morris and Wolseley range of cars, and it certainly did not have the pedigree of, say, an Aston Martin. That snobbery remains today and TA and TB are not accepted into the ranks of the Vintage Sports Car Club, other than in a very basic standard form. Such cars would be totally uncompetitive at a VSCC race meeting. This is one of the reasons why in the late 1960s T-type owners formed their own racing series. But we are getting a bit ahead of ourselves…

The TB was produced into the first weeks of World War II, before the factory was given over to weapons production. Many of the TB chassis propped up against the walls of the factory through the war would form the basis of the postwar T-type. The TB is the rarest of the T-types, and if the cart-sprung cars appeal to you - ie the TA, TB or TC – the TB is really the model to own.

TB Driving Impressions

I bought TB 0594 in 1968 and got it on the road in 1972, only parting with it in 2004. It went through several stages of engine tune since I first fitted a 1250cc Wolseley XPAW, and was finally bored out to 1370cc, or 0.120in oversize, which is the maximum size you can take an XPAG engine to without having to bore it out completely and fit cylinder liners.

In addition the car was fitted with what is termed a stage 2 cylinder head with a 9:1 compression ratio, polished ports and 1½in carburettors. These were mounted on a Derrington extractor manifold which I originally bought in 1969. The exhaust system on this car was non-standard as well, being of wider bore and fitted with two small "cherrybomb" silencers. The exhaust was mounted so that it could rotate – the manifold itself could rotate

The one-piece seat back was common to all T-types until the TF, which had individual seats. On the steering column can be seen the clamp for adjusting the length of the column. This was introduced in 1938. The wheel itself is the popular Bluemels "Brooklands" type, with four sprung spokes and the pre-war black rim. These wheels were not supplied by the factory.

MG T SERIES IN DETAIL

The Monaco MG as offered by P R Monkhouse. It was based on the TB, with engine enlarged to 1385cc.

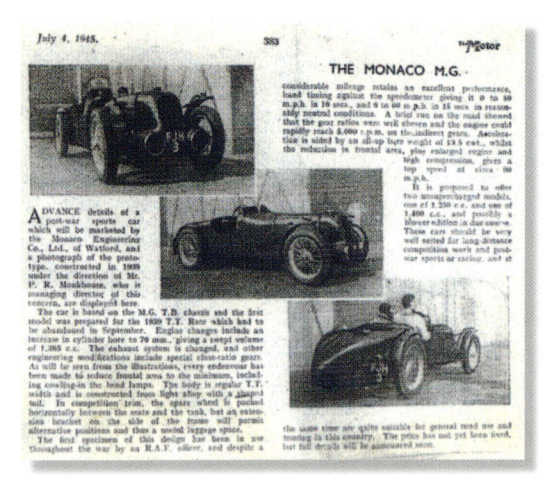

The standard tonneau cover, optional luggage rack, and a clever way of fitting direction indicators without spoiling the period feel.

inside the exhaust pipe to absorb some of the twisting effects of engine torque, and the pipe was suspended on rubber mountings.

The dashboard was modified so that the speedometer was in front of the driver and to the right of the speedometer was a small 4-inch Smiths electronic rev counter. The horn button/dipswitch was in the normal place, but just below it and slightly to its right was an indicator switch. The slow-running control was disconnected although it was all there, and the two-pin socket for auxiliary lighting, etc., was in place, but to the left of that and the ignition warning light were three switches: one for a spotlight, one for the side and headlights and the left-hand one for the ignition. The original ignition and lighting switch was removed and replaced by a water temperature gauge, which sat between the ammeter and the oil pressure gauge.

The car was started by a push-switch to a solenoid, which then operated the smaller starter motor found on the TD and TF and the Wolseley 4/44. The choke was pulled out to the maximum and could immediately be pushed home once the engine has started, whereupon it would idle smoothly at around 1000rpm.

On the road the first thing you noticed was the considerable pulling power of the engine, which developed 75-80bhp and had a very wide torque band. The car therefore had ample acceleration for modern traffic conditions, in second and third gears especially,

The steering was excellent and does not reflect the general perception of the Bishop Cam steering gear in the TA, TB and TC range. The box was never rebuilt while I owned the

64

The 16-inch wheels on the TB fill up the wheel arches as well as the larger standard wheels and in the author's opinion improve the car's looks.

car, but it was well maintained and regularly topped up with EP140 oil. Proper attention was paid to correct adjustment of the track rod ends, as well as to spring location, castor angle and camber angle. Even at low speeds the steering was light, and those used to power steering would only notice the lack of it in tight parking conditions. The best way to handle a TA, TB or TC is to hold the steering wheel very lightly and let the car and the steering work for you. Like all the early T-types the steering was very direct and a small turn of the wheel had quite a significant effect on directional stability. This particular car could be driven one-handed with one finger resting on the spokes.

The suspension was hard, and not rough as a long as you didn't have any loose objects in the car. It rode silently over quite enormous bumps, especially around the roads of North Bedfordshire where I live, some of which don't appear to have been maintained properly since the Middle Ages! The car ran flat and true, and swift progress could be made on not only A or B roads but also unmarked roads. Like most MGs the car had a degree of understeer built into it, but this particular one, with the extra 20 or so horsepower, could be balanced well on the throttle, making cornering a delight and opening the eyes of many a hot hatch behind.

The car involved you, and although at one time it was fitted with a radio, this was really for static purposes only, as you don't need ICE in cars of this nature; the music of the engine and the rush of the wind and cries of nature are all you do need. The hood was rarely erected, and a TB is a very different beast to drive with the hood up. This was only done *in extremis*, for instance heavy rain that does not look as if it is going to stop within five minutes. Then it was best always to take out the driver's sidescreen to minimise condensation, especially when on roads which are flooded as a lot of steam can come off the exhaust pipe into the cockpit. These MGs are not insulated like modern cars, and the ingress of steam and the smell of burnt mud are things one would always associate with them.

The cylinder head on my TB was modified for unleaded fuel but was rarely actually run on it, there being a nearby outlet for full four-star leaded petrol in the area. The exhaust smelt considerably sweeter when it was running on four-star as against unleaded and the engine ran a little bit cooler as well, while the corrosive effects of unleaded petrol were avoided. In the past, using unleaded fuel, the float chambers had the solder stripped out of them and some of the rubber washers holding the floats to the carburettors were rotted.

The TB that is the subject of the Driving Impressions in this chapter. It has a 1370cc engine and was the author's car from 1968 to 2004. This picture was taken in Wales in 1998.

65

Chapter Four

The TC

Two views of the TC exhibited at the 1946 motor show. Ten years after the introduction of the TA, there is no great visual difference between the two models.

Before studying the TC's career, it might be appropriate to look back to the beginning of the T series and the people who were involved in its design and production. Up to 1935 Abingdon had its own drawing office, but this was closed down and all the drawing office staff were transferred to Morris Motors at Cowley, accompanied by H N Charles, the chief designer. Cecil Cousins, a long-time MG employee, has gone on record as stating that the first car to come out of the Morris Motors drawing office was the SA and that the first Midget was the TA. Fortunately there were still easy relationships between the two factories, and while the TA was in gestation Cecil Kimber would keep popping in and out of the Cowley office, commenting on aspects of its design. Yet it would be fair to say that the principal designer of the TA was H N Charles. Syd Enever probably led the input from Abingdon and Kimber – still unquestionably the boss – was ultimately responsible for the project. The TA was the last Midget to receive real Kimber input, and this would have been carried through into the design of the TB and the TC, as these three cars were all fundamentally similar.

During the war car production was suspended, though there will have been unused TB chassis left in the factory. Cecil Kimber left MG during this period and, as is well known, was killed in a freak train accident on 4 February 1945. A new managing director, H A Ryder, had been appointed after Kimber's departure. Previously he had been a director of the Morris Radiator Company and was a very clever engineer, but he had never made a car or worked with anybody who had. However, as well as being an engineer he was a very skilled hands-on mechanic and a wonderful sheet metal worker.

There was of course discussion after the war about what cars should be made. Ryder thought that the factory should resume production of the TB, but the suggestion was made that it would be better first to make a study of the TB's weaker points and then improve it. The pre-war records were examined: the main points which emerged were that the car was not wide enough, and that the sliding trunnions on the road springs were the most expensive and most frequent service item. As a result, the TC received a body four inches wider between the rear door pillars. This enlarged the cockpit width also by four inches, giving considerably more elbow room. The body type number was changed from B270 to B280. The sliding trunnions were replaced by rubber shackles, and the TC model was announced in October 1945. Eighty-one cars were made before the end of 1945.

There were other major changes to the car. New Luvax-Girling shock absorbers were fitted of the double-acting piston type, rather than previous the vane-type Luvax units. The 6-volt

Overleaf: This TC is chassis number TC 8315, an Export model first registered in May 1949 and brought back to Britain in November 1950. It belongs to Eric Nicholls.

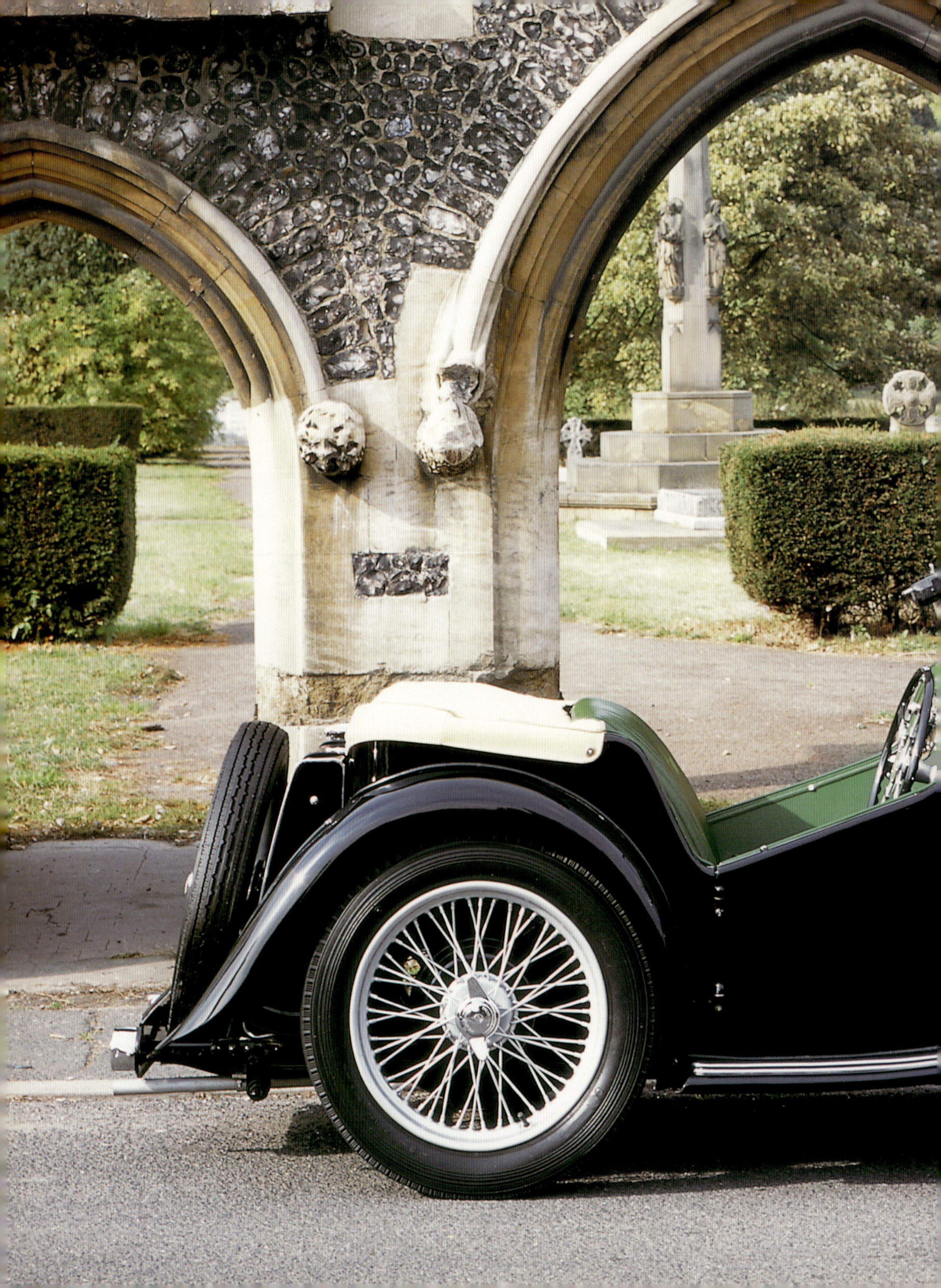

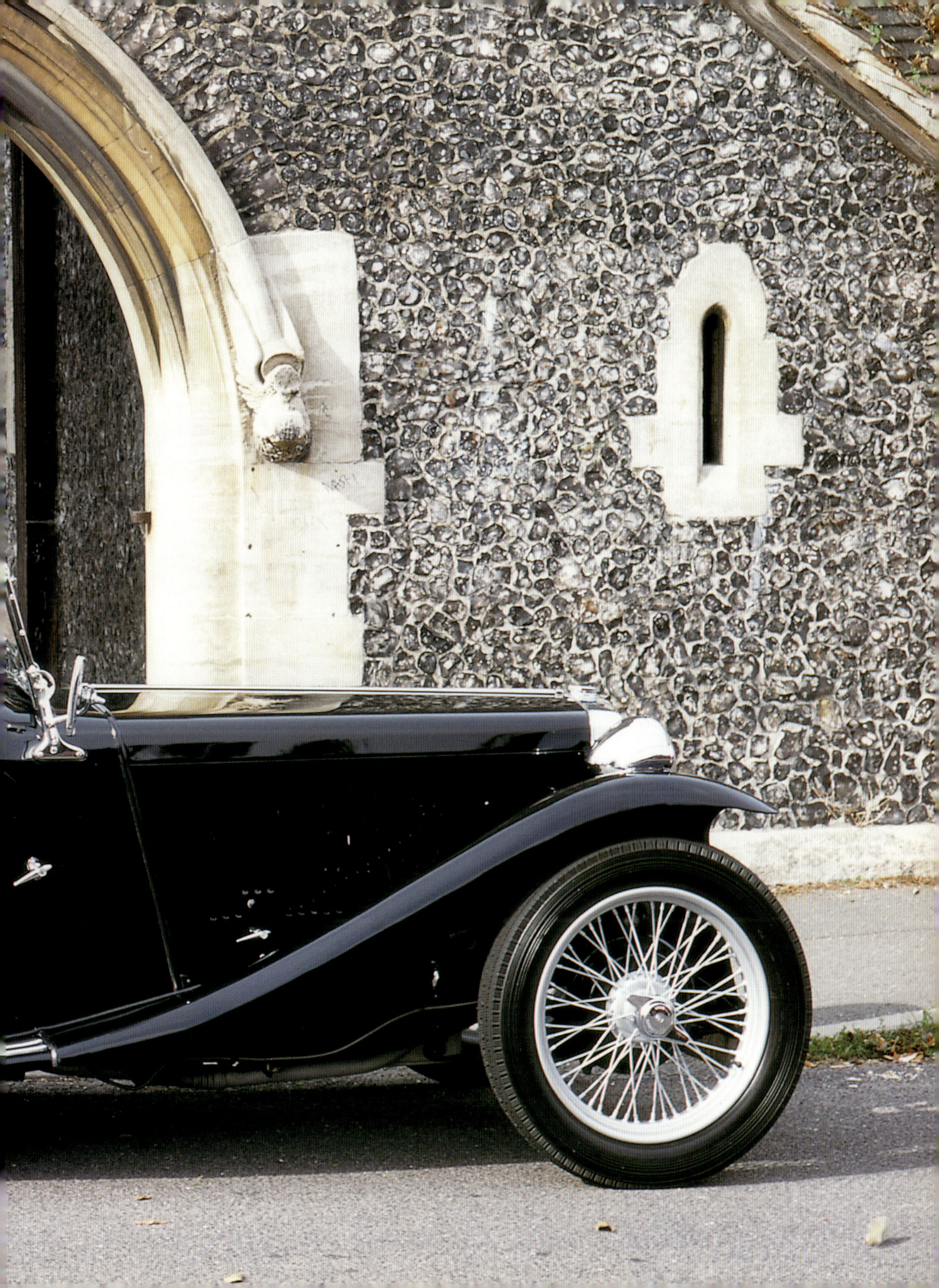

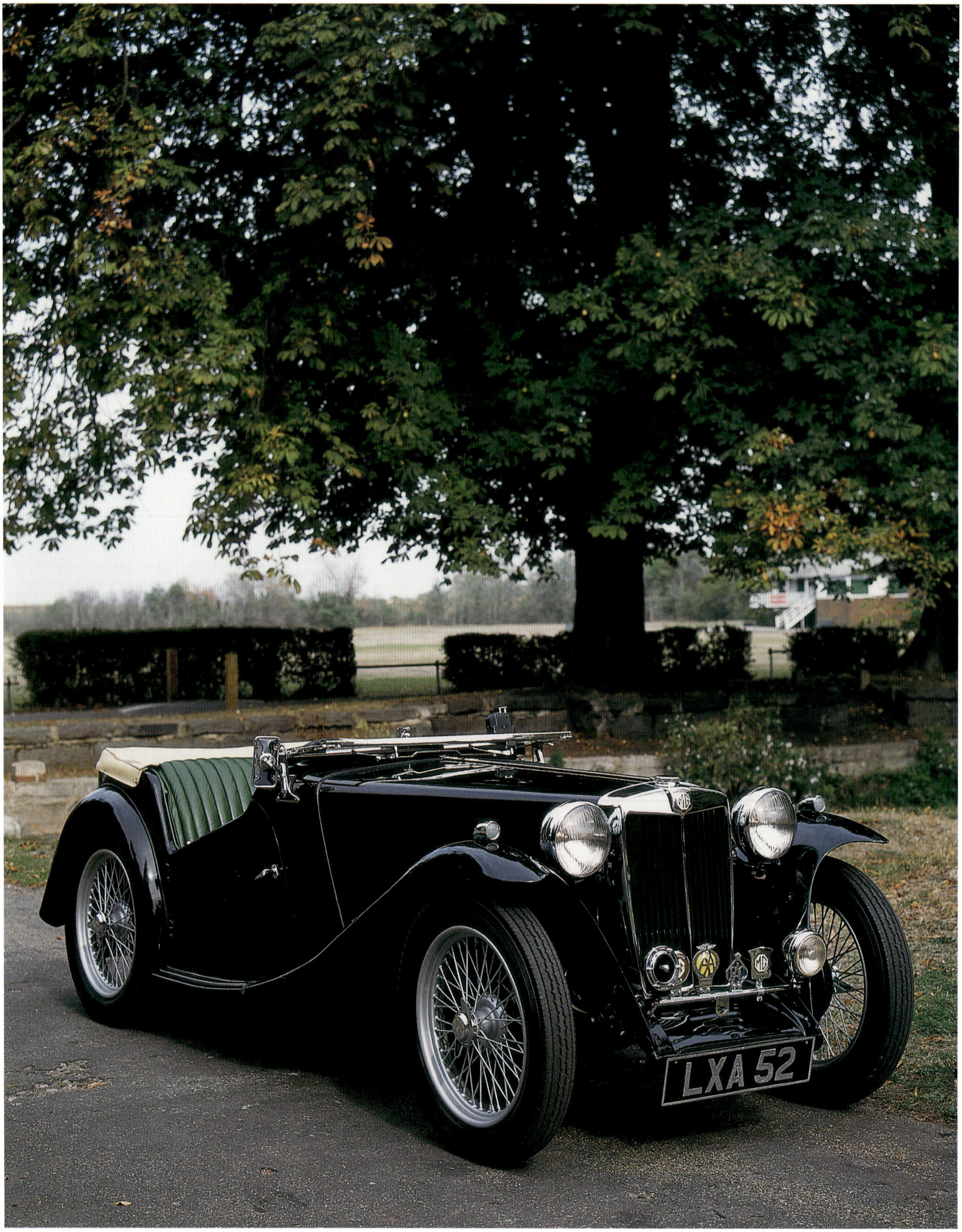
LXA 52

batteries behind the seats were dispensed with and instead a single 12-volt battery was mounted in a much more accessible position on the bulkhead in a separate steel container. Behind the battery box was a narrow metal toolbox which was accessible from both sides of the car. It was closed by sprung up-and-over catches and was lined with felt, but there was no longer a top tray to hold spanners.

The instruments were updated and the Jaeger green-faced dials were standardised. A low fuel warning light was fitted in place of the fuel reserve switch of the pre-war cars, and thus a single fuel line replaced the dual lines. The dash retained a map reading light, and a 30mph warning light.

The under-bonnet appearance was improved, with electrical leads and pipe lines neatly arranged, and early engines were painted a greenish-grey before giving way to a deep MG maroon.

The very early TCs came in Black – shades of Henry Ford though obviously caused by postwar supply difficulties – but colours later available included MG Red, Regency Red, Shires Green, Almond Green, Ivory and Clipper Blue. Unlike the TA and TB, the paint options for the TC were restricted to single colours. Although you may see TCs these days painted in a duotone scheme, this was never original. The 19-inch wheels, which were now all centre laced, were painted silver and the radiator slat

The headlamp glass pattern remained the same as on the TA and TB.

Opposite: The more sharply pointed front wings are a distinguishing feature from pre-war cars.

71

TCs in production at the Abingdon factory in the late 1940s, with a line of YA saloons alongside. The basic layout of the shop floor hardly changed from the earliest days to the close of production.

colour usually matched the interior colour.

The XPAG engine gained a timing chain tensioner, together with a new camshaft front cover to accommodate it, and the tappet chest cover was redesigned so that it was less prone to cutting the large rectangular cork gasket which sealed it from the oil draining down from the cylinder head via the push rod tubes. Between engine numbers XPAG2020 and XPAG2965 a polished aluminium rocker cover with a nicely engineered flip-top oil filler cap was introduced as standard equipment. However, it was obviously too expensive to make, and the later cars, like the ones prior to engine number XPAG2020, were fitted with a pressed steel rocker cover.

The standard TC has had its performance figures published in all sorts of publications and they always end up as being the following:

0-30mph	5.7 seconds
0-40mph	8.8 seconds
0-50mph	14 seconds
0-60mph	21 seconds
0-70mph	33.3 seconds
Standing quarter mile	21.8 seconds

Maximum speed was 73mph and average petrol consumption 25mpg. These figures were obtained from a fully road-equipped TC with hood and sidescreens fitted. The author would dispute the 25mpg fuel consumption, which in his experience was much nearer to 30 mpg and on long, relatively uninterrupted journeys as much as 33-35mpg.

The gearbox first fitted to the TB was retained. This is a marvellous unit, immensely strong. It was much sought-after by special builders, especially in the United States were it was often mated to a flathead Ford V8 engine and successfully dealt with power outputs in excess of 100bhp. In modern times, when some racing XPAG engines produce 140bhp or more, this gearbox is perfectly capable of handling the additional power and torque.

The road springs were slightly longer than on the TA and the TB, with fewer leaves, and imparted the car with a softer ride. I recall changing my TA for a TC in 1962 and gaining the distinct impression that the TC was a "bouncier" car. Indeed when I took it racing in 1963/64, despite the TC's reputation for being very stiff and cornering flat, I was able to generate enormous roll angles between the body and the chassis under those racing conditions. The inside rear wheel would lift clear of the ground in a corner and the car quickly lost its rubber bump stops! On the road, however, the TC was a major advance over the TA and TB in terms of driver and passenger comfort. The extra cockpit width reduced the previously enforced intimacy between driver and passenger.

Although the TA, TB and TC all appear to have similar brake master cylinders, there is a subtle difference in that the TC master cylinder has a slightly shorter canister compared to the TA and TB. The master cylinders on all these cars are in a very vulnerable position, exposed to road dirt and spray, and it is necessary to dismantle the assemblies from time to time in order to clean them. In this day and age a lot of T-types are only occasionally used and the danger is that while they are laid up, the brake fluid, which is highly hygroscopic, goes sticky up in the wheel cylinders, causing pistons to seize and eventual leakages.

It is therefore important to devote regular maintenance to the braking system so as to avoid premature failure. Some owners have switched from regular brake fluid to silicone fluid, which avoids the hygroscopic problem. If you do this the system should at the least be thoroughly flushed, and preferably all pipes and seals should be replaced. Use methylated spirit to flush out the system. The author is not convinced that silicone fluid is the answer. It seems to work with simple systems like the T-types', but MGB owners report problems with it destroying seals, especially in the servo. Those who race T-types use conventional fluid to a high specification.

The interior on the early TCs retained leather seats and leather door trims; the rest of the trim was in Rexine, which could be described as an early vinyl material. Fairly early in the TC production, probably during 1947, possibly 1948, the leather door trims were replaced by Rexine, but the pattern was exactly the same.

The gearbox cover was a one-piece rubber moulding, exactly the same as on the TB but different from the TA's due to the different dimensions of the gearbox. The carpeting was as before: a short-pile black carpet laid on felt and secured by lift-off fasteners. The dimensions of the front carpets in the TC would probably have been exactly the same as those in the TB and later TAs with the narrower body. The leather seat back however, is wider than that on the TB and TA due to the extra width of the body when measured across the rear door pillars. Although a TC seat back will fit into a TA or TB the sides will chafe against the hood.

There were some minor bodywork changes during the production run. The early cars had front wings identical to those used on the TB and the late TA, which had a deep cut back on the leading edge between the tip at the front and the chassis. Later on the depth of this cut back was reduced and the tip of the wing assumed a more pointed shape.

The first TCs had a walnut-veneered dashboard but during 1948 this was changed a plywood dash covered in Rexine to match the

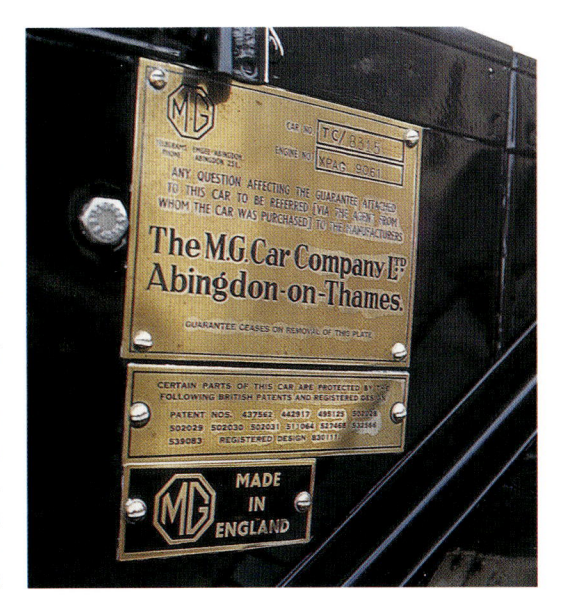

Being an Export model, this car has an additional "Made in England" plate.

A restored TC chassis. Note the circular pinion flange: on the TA and TB the flange was square.

A TC body tub, still built of wood and iron, with outer panels nailed on, at a time when pressed steel bodies were the norm.

MG T SERIES IN DETAIL

The TC body is 4½ inches wider at the door hinge pillars than the earlier cars. Thus the running boards are narrower and only have two tread strips in place of three.

For the TC the twin six-volt batteries slung either side of the propshaft were replaced by a single 12-volt battery relocated to the engine compartment, with the toolboxes behind.

colour of the upholstery. At the same time the steel instrument panel supplied by Lucas, on early TCs black with white lettering, was changed to tan with black lettering. A flat Rexine-covered hardboard panel ran from the bottom of the dashboard to the bulkhead and neatly hid the wiring. Very few cars now possess this piece of equipment. Most of them were discarded in the 1960s and 1970s, when the wiring of the cars became old and in need of frequent attention!

The hood and sidescreens were of double duck in a tan colour. Early TCs had divided rear windows but these were later replaced by a single flexible panel. The original tonneau covers were either black or tan and that usually remains the case to this day.

The original price of the TC in 1945 was £375, which had increased to £412.10s by 1949. Factory options were limited to a luggage carrier and Radiomobile radio, which was installed under the dashboard. This was not much of an options list when you consider that for the TA and TB you could have a bonnet strap, a cigarette lighter, a full-length tonneau cover with a zipper, a radio, an oil thermometer and a second spare wheel option. The period after the war in the 1950s saw an expansion in aftermarket equipment for cars and the TC was no exception in attracting the attention of the salesmen of the period. In America in particular there were many various and wonderful accessories, and gradually, as the UK became a little more affluent, a full range of products was available in this country. You could have extra gauges, all sorts of tuning equipment, superchargers, stage two cylinder heads or aluminium cylinder heads, extractor exhaust manifolds, aluminium rocker and tappet covers, radiator muffs, driving lights, Alfin brake drums, wind

This hood has the correct pattern of split rear window.

Early TCs had a handsome cast alloy rocker cover like this one, but for reasons of cost this was soon changed to a pressed steel cover.

Because of the repositioning of the battery the TC's under-bonnet toolbox was much narrower. It was lined with off-white felt.

deflectors, different headlamps, indicators, sun visors, different steering wheels, the Bluemels being the most popular and long lasting, although during the 1960s and '70s the writer recalls wood-rim aluminium-spoked steering wheels being offered for the TC, as well as the later TD and TF. The list could go on endlessly but the important thing to remember is that very few of these aftermarket items were available from the factory.

As the 1940s grew towards the 1950s, the TC began to sell in far greater quantities than pre-war, and it became a familiar sight on the road as a daily car, gracing city car parks and rural market places in equal profusion. It became something of a fashion icon in its day. In 1947 Prince Phillip acquired one. Other famous owners included the novelists Ernest Hemingway and John O'Hara, and several found their way to Hollywood, although their owners' motives for buying a TC might be wondered at, like Rocky Marciano! John Thornley called the MG K3 the epitome of the MG and certainly that would be true of the racing models and perhaps all of the pre-war MGs, but the TC is the car that really epitomises MG so far as the general public is concerned.

By 1950, when the last of the cars were produced, 10,000 had been sold, many of them for export, with a large proportion of those going to the United States. After the Americans joined the war and came in large numbers over to Europe, many servicemen were attracted by the little MG. Some picked up TAs and TBs and took them home after the war. One or two of them opened dealerships, leading to the establishment of a network of MG dealers in the United States and the growth of the number of TCs sold there in the final years of the 1940s.

Although in Britain there was a postwar slogan "Export or Die", it may come as a surprise that only 2001 TCs were actually exported to the United States – some say only 1820. This might be the difference between official figures released by the MG Car Company and more unofficial figures, perhaps generated in the United States, including cars that were personally imported, having been purchased privately in the UK or in Europe. In addition, TCs did not start to arrive in America until 1948 in any quantity. The cars were also exported elsewhere, with Australia receiving 27 per cent, South Africa 9 per cent, Switzerland 6 per cent and Belgium 4 per cent. Apart from the major markets listed above, cars found their way into Rhodesia, Canada, India, Pakistan, Argentina, Brazil, Eire, West Germany, Ceylon, Egypt, Hong Kong and Sweden. One or two of them even penetrated the Iron Curtain. Between 1945 and 1949, 74 per cent of all TCs constructed were exported.

The reason why the TC was considered such an excellent competition car in the late 1940s and early 1950s was its roadholding and handling as well as the extra power that could

The TC did not have the previous models' moulded tool trays. Instead a tool roll was supplied.

Offside of the TC engine, showing the new position of the control box. The petrol reserve set-up of the TA and TB was replaced by a low fuel level warning lamp.

Nearside of the engine. Most TCs had this painted pressed steel rocker cover, and the identification plates have moved compared with the earlier cars.

be extracted by tuning the XPAG engine. A number of racing drivers of the 1950s and '60s cut their teeth on TCs, including Peter Arundel and Peter Taylor, Phil Hill, Carole Shelby, Ritchie Ginther and John Fitch; Ken Miles also raced a TC before developing his famous specials. In England, apart from Peter Arundel and Peter Taylor, drivers such as Dick Jacobs, Ted Lund and George Phillips, then a photographer for *Autosport*, were driving works-prepared TCs. George Phillips went on to race a special-bodied TC at Le Mans in 1949 and in 1950, when he finished second in the 1.5-litre class.

Mention has already been made of the TC/EXU. There were other variations. Obviously the most common version was the home model as described, but then there was also a general export model identified as the TC/EXR – "E" for export and "R" for right hand drive, and it was this model which was shipped in large numbers to all parts of the world. There was then a sub-type, known as the TC/EXR/K, which had its speedometer calibrated in kilometres per hour.

The TC/EXU differed in many ways from the home and EXR models. Firstly it was fitted with bumpers, presumably in response to demand from "contact parkers"! They were rather cumbersome items which altered the appearance of the car quite considerably, and many owners dispensed with them. They can be recognised by the MG medallion in the middle of the rear bumper. Two Lucas Windtone Horns were mounted under the bonnet. While the home model had lettering for the switches on the central dash panel, there was none on the EXU panel.

Indicators were not fitted to the T-types leaving Abingdon, hand signals being the norm, but the TC/EXU had a turn signal circuit added to the wiring. The signals were controlled by a Lucas SD84 rotary switch, situated on the instrument panel in place of the inspection lamp socket. The front side lights and the rear lamps served as the indicators, and one of the quirks of this design was that the front side lamp filaments lit up every time the driver hit the brakes. The rear number plate lamp was mounted centrally above the rear bumper with Lucas number plate lights above it. The TC/EXU also did away with the D-lamps fitted next to the rear number plate, which were replaced by two Lucas 482-1 lamps mounted high on the end panels of the fuel tank.

The headlamps on the home market cars were still single dipping, but on the TC/EXR and TC/EXU double dipping was the norm, the TC/EXU having smaller S700 Lucas headlamps, similar to those that appeared on the TD, in place of the standard Lucas M140 headlamps. The S700 headlamps were of 7in diameter compared with the 8in M140 units. The TC/EXU was not fitted with a front fog lamp, and the fog lamp switch was replaced a high beam warning light.

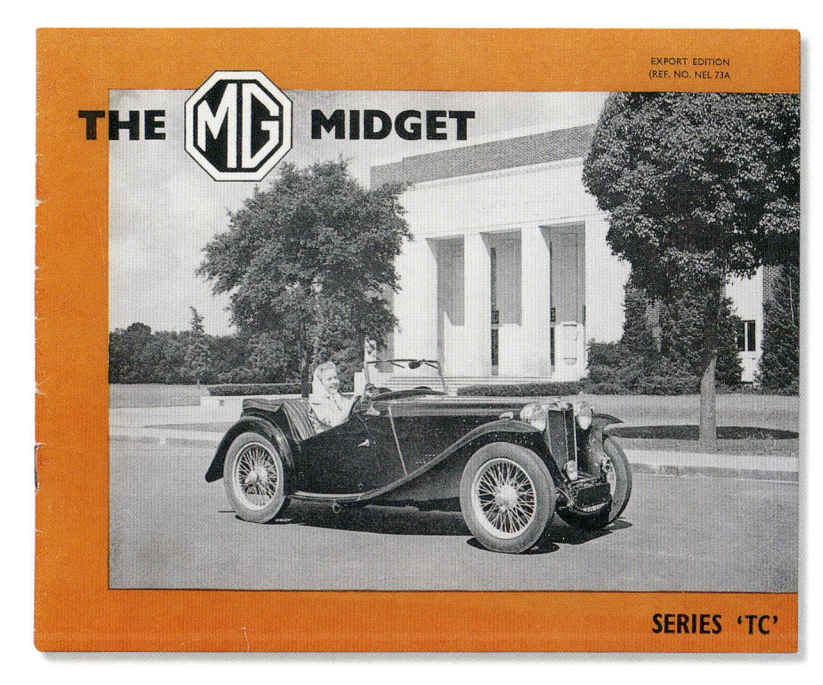

The home market car and the EXR cars incorporated a 30mph warning light, fitted in place of the driver's side map light. It was wired to the speedometer, which had internal contacts enabling this light to light up at about 20mph and go out again just over 30mph. The EXU model did not have this lamp fitted and had an ordinary map reading light in its place. A rear view mirror was fitted to EXU cars in the centre of the instrument cowl whereas home market

Front cover of the export edition of the TC brochure.

Two appealing pages from the TC brochure, offering more faithful reproductions of the shape of the car than had been common before the war. The "10.9" on the number plates refers to the engine's RAC horsepower rating.

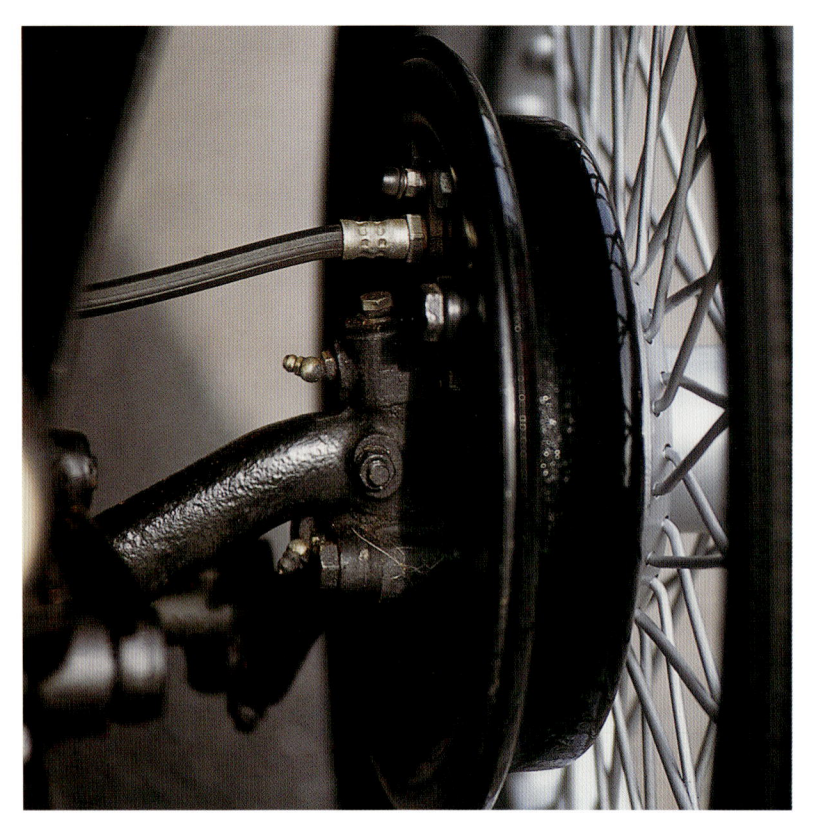

Single leading shoe hydraulic front brake with its 9-inch steel drum.

The pedals, with the roller-type accelerator and the rubber fume excluder at the base of the brake and clutch stalks. Note the easy access to the gearbox filler and the top of the gearbox dipstick.

Opposite: During 1948 TCs began to receive Rexine-covered dashboards, coloured to match the interior trim.

cars didn't have interior mirrors, and the windscreens of the EXU cars were laminated as against toughened on the other models.

The TC/EXU steering wheel was different from the standard black home market item and usually had a tan and gold pearl rim, with chrome-plated steel spokes. There was no provision for left-hand drive.

Only 494 TC/EXUs were produced, starting with chassis number TC EXU 7380 in December 1948. How many now exist is not known but maybe the same percentage as surviving TBs. A genuine TC/EXU has the full identification number stamped on the chassis and also on the guarantee plate on the bulkhead.

Early in the TC's production it had no real rivals other than those cars mentioned in the chapters on the TA and TB. However, all this changed in 1948 when Jaguar introduced the XK120 with its six-cylinder twin overhead cam engine. It was considerably more comfortable and powerful than the TC, but more relevant to the TC's future was that it heralded a completely new era in sports car design, signalling the slow but inexorable demise of the T-type and the classic Ulster style. This was the beginning of the end not only for the T-type but also for some of its contemporaries.

Factory-backed competition had all but ceased and there were no Cream Cracker or Musketeer teams of TC trials cars. In 1949/50 the birth pangs of the BMC competition department could be felt and three TCs were raced, by Dick Jacobs, Ted Lund and George Phillips, with some tacit works backing. Unfortunately there seems to be no record of these cars' registration numbers. They had to be raced virtually as standard on 19in wheels and it is unlikely that the engines received any tuning other than very careful assembly and balancing.

In all, 10,000 TCs were manufactured between October 1945 and the end of 1949. This was a threefold increase on TA production, and it was the TC above all other cars that introduced America to sports car motoring and changed the way of life of so many of its owners.

The standard TC with its clamshell wings and tall, thin wheels has lyrically been described as "a coffin riding on harps". It is certainly one of the great designs of the 20th century and, amidst the blandness of modern car design, is instantly recognisable. It also shares the characteristic of many MG models that if you own one you are possibly driving it at a profit, as their values increase or at worst remain stable. Finally, a well sorted TA, TB, TC, TD or TF is very cheap to run.

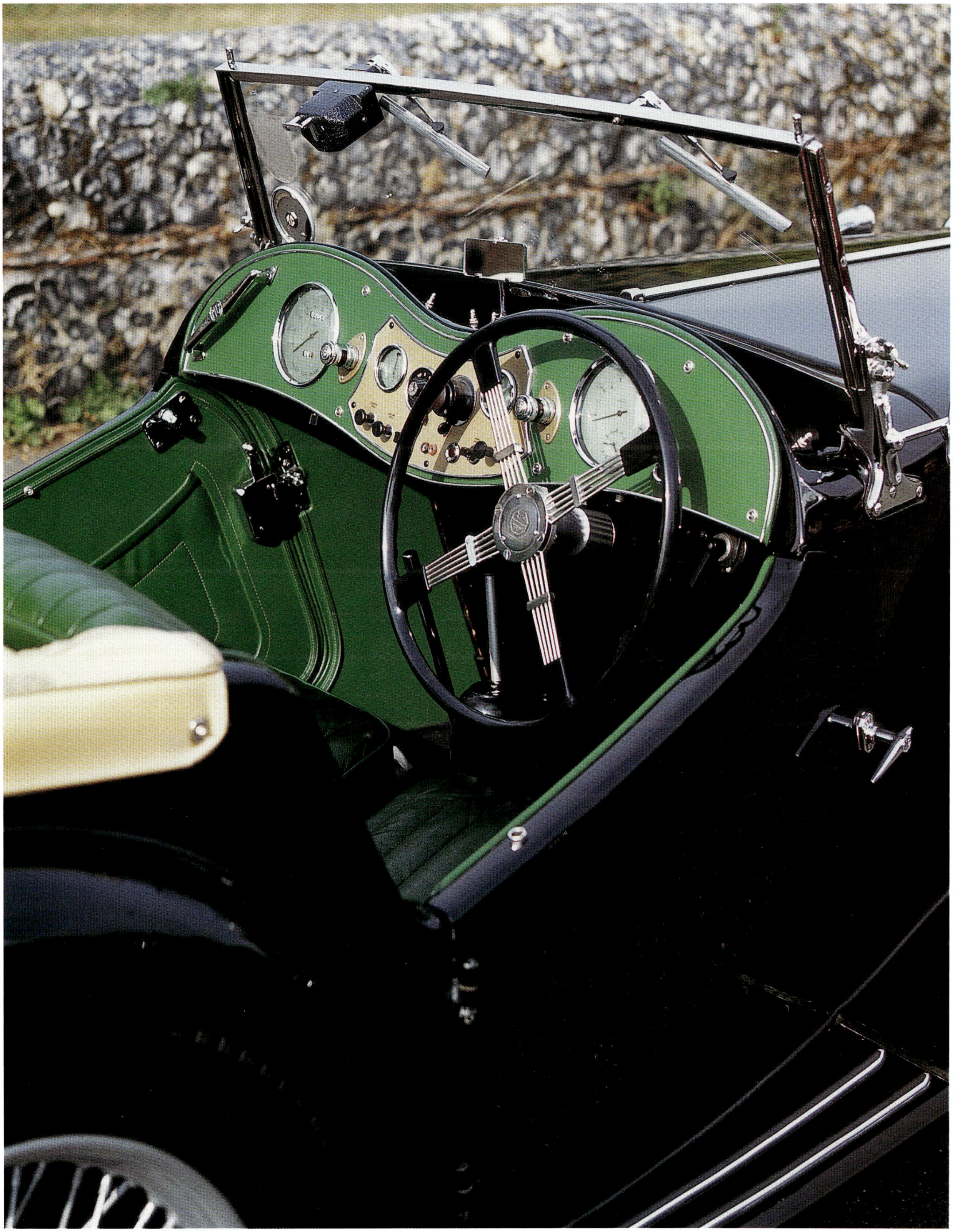

MG T SERIES IN DETAIL

The nicely trimmed cockpit of Eric Nicholls's TC, with the single-piece seat back carried over from pre-war models. This car too has the Bluemels "Brooklands" steering wheel.

During 1948 the colour of the central instrument panel on the TC changed from black to this sandy bronze colour.

Facing page: Racing at Watkins Glen, USA, September 16 1951. Paul P Ramos in his TC has Robert J Wilder's Allard J2 close on his tail.

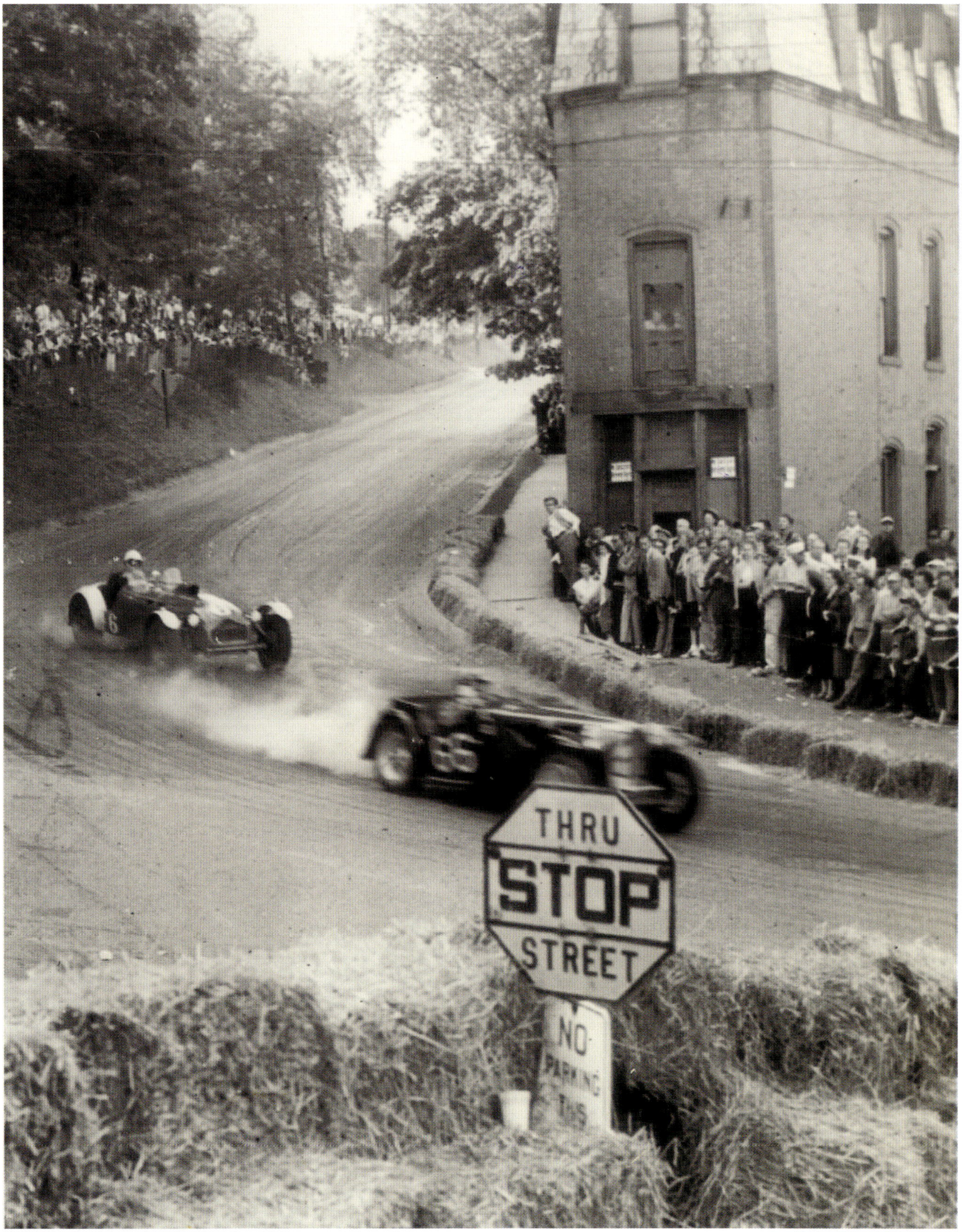
THRU
STOP
STREET
NO
PARKING
THIS

A full tonneau cover was not standard equipment but could be ordered as an extra.

Stowage for the sidescreens behind the seats.

TC Driving Impressions

I was lucky enough to test-drive two TCs, Peter Jones's relatively early 1946 one, and a mid-production TC belonging to Julian White.

I sampled Peter's car first and was immediately struck by how high you sit in the cockpit when the seats are virtually new. Peter is quite tall and I would not be surprised if he actually looks over the windscreen when driving. The steering wheel is the Bluemels four-spoke plastic-rim accessory of the time and the dashboard has some additional instruments in it, including a boost gauge for a supercharger. Currently the car is un-supercharged but a few years ago it was fitted with a Shorrocks unit. The water temperature gauge on the right hand side of the dash came out of an American wartime bomber.

The engine is bored out to 1348cc and fitted with Powermax pistons, having been constructed in the mid-1970s. It was stripped about a year later when Peter fitted an AEG 122 camshaft, and the engine has been in the car ever since, other than having its big ends replaced a couple of times in the intervening years. It is fitted with the standard 7¼in clutch and drives through a Riley RME series gearbox, which has slightly different and lower ratios from the standard TC 'box, but this is compensated for by the fitting of a 4.67:1 final drive. The wheels are standard 19-inch fitted with 450x19 tyres.

The suspension has been raised, although it has lowered itself slightly through natural wear as Peter uses the car not only for general road driving but also for trials. It has regularly competed in all the MCC Classic Trials, such as The Lands End, The Exeter and The Edinburgh for very many years. Peter also raced the car for one year in the T Register's Drivers Championsip, in the standard class, so it is indeed a car for all seasons.

The engine fires up instantly with a little bit of choke, before returning an even idle.

The pedals are close together and it was necessary for me to change from a pair of boots into a narrower pair of shoes to be able to drive easily. On setting off, the gears changed easily, the gearbox was relatively silent and it was necessary to keep my foot off the clutch altogether as otherwise I induced clutch slip.

Although the TC is wider than the TB, paradoxically there is less room in the footwell.

The Bishop Cam steering was excellent, responsive and the car very stable over the bumpy single-track roads I tested it on in mid-Wales. On the main A44 it pulled well in top gear, cruising easily at 60mph. The suspension on the TC, as previously noted, is softer than on the TA and TB, and this was quite noticeable. The car certainly gives a more comfortable ride than my old TB. The brakes were sharp and they were reassuring on the steep hills encountered.

It was a misty sort of a day and the windscreen wipers worked effectively, although on

Aeroscreens were another frequently fitted item

A TC, with panniers strapped to its luggage rack, takes a lonely road on the 1953 Daily Express Rally.

the passenger side there is a large vertical crack in the windscreen with a corresponding darkening of the laminate each side which does obscure the passenger's view. The car was driven without any side screens and there was considerable buffeting above 50mph, which could be uncomfortable over a longer distance, especially in the cold weather at the end of November!

Although the car didn't smoke much there is the occasional blue puff typical of an engine fitted with Powermax pistons, and Peter confirmed to me that it did use quite a lot of oil.

After stopping at the local Post Office we set off into the wilds, and the road included climbing a very steep hill with a sharp right-hand turn at it steepest point. The TC romped up the slope and was able to round this corner still in second gear, in which we remained until the gradient levelled off and I was able to change up. There is more of a gap between second and third on the Riley 'box.

Soon the road dropped steeply into a valley. It was then that the car exhibited a somewhat disconcerting habit of jumping out of third gear on the overrun, so that I had to steer one-handed while holding the gear lever in place. This is a common failing of TC gearboxes (and Riley ones, it seems) and was a phenomenon that I frequently encountered when racing my car, so that I am almost subconsciously aware of the moment that it jumps out of gear even if I don't rev the engine.

I then changed cars and took the wheel of Julian's TC. This example has also had quite a history, as initially he raced it very successfully in the T Register Drivers Championship for many years, not without the occasional crash. When he retired from racing, Julian converted it back into a trials car, raising the suspension a bit and fitting a stainless steel exhaust which passes over the rear chassis crossmember. Like Peter's car, this one has a skid under the brake master cylinder. Incidentally, Peter's favourite piece of exhaust for trials was a section of scaffold pipe!

The engine in Julian's TC is also bored out to 1348cc but is fitted with the later Acralite forged three-ring pistons, which don't consume as much oil as the Powermax pistons. It has a very neat supercharger conversion, comprising a Magnusson supercharger, made in the United States, which has a very period look to it and is fitted with a 1¾in SU carburettor and a KN air cleaner. The supercharger is driven by twin belts and the dashboard incorporates a boost gauge. Julian built the engine that is currently in the car in the 1980s and it too is fitted with an AEG 122 camshaft.

The car is fitted with cycle wings front and rear, the front wings having additional side spats attached to the inside edge to avoid the worst of the wet weather and spray, but nonetheless on a long wet drive the driver's elbow can get very wet.

The standard TC gearbox is fitted and the back axle is a converted TC axle fitted with a Ford differential and appropriately modified half shafts. The wheels are 19-inch and are shod with 450 Michelin Bibendum tyres, which, with their chunky tread, Julian finds good for trials use.

The engine starts easily but the supercharger has become somewhat noisy at low revs. I was immediately faced with a steep climb up to the top to the moor. Working hard, the supercharger whined splendidly, providing ample torque and revs to romp up the hill, which involved a sharp left-hand turn at almost its steepest point, and the TC then proceeded very crisply to climb the rest of the hill using a combination of second and third gears. The narrower gap between these ratios and the extra power made this climb easier, so that I was able to catch Peter's car, which had set off in front of us..

All TCs had this pear-shaped gear gear knob.

MG T SERIES IN DETAIL

The two TCs tested by the author. The green car is Julian White's supercharged car with cycle wings, and Peter Jone's car is the red one.

Again the Bishop Cam steering was excellent, with good directional stability at all times. Julian had fitted a Bluemels steering wheel, this time with a black rim. He had fitted a Datsun steering box a few years earlier, which I had sampled then and was expecting this time, I had not liked it as it was low geared and not as sensitive to road conditions as the original. Julian had found the same, and we were both happy that the car now had a standard 'box.

On the main A44 the TC accelerated briskly, and it provided me with an exhilarating drive home behind its 1350 supercharged engine, which brought back a lot of memories. At high speeds I found the 19-inch tyres somewhat skittish, especially on a slippery right-hand bend when the back end slipped slightly out of line, but this was easily corrected.

Summing up, Peter's car is probably the more user-friendly, but for sheer fun there is little to beat the supercharger set-up that Julian has on his car. Although I drove his car with no side screens, it was fitted with wind deflectors on each side of the windscreen, similar to the ones that I had on my TB, and these do reduce the buffeting effect quite considerably. Julian's car also had twin aeroscreens behind the windscreen which I found slightly impeded visibility. I imagine they would cause difficulty in damp conditions, especially when the hood is up, as condensation easily forms on the inside of the windscreen, and could coat both sides of the aeroscreens as well. Both cars are fitted with full weather equipment – side screens, hood and tonneau cover – but in the true spirit of T-type driving these are rarely used. The oil pressures on both cars was similar, at 50-60psi, dropping slightly on idle.

If this account of driving a delightful pair of TCs has whetted anybody's appetite, now is the time to buy, as prices have come down considerably and, at the time of writing, are at their lowest for several years.

The nearside of the engine in Peter's car, showing the spin-off oil filter conversion and the rev counter drive on the back of the dynamo.

By contrast the engine bay of Julian's TC is filled with the supercharger. This is a modern unit but it has a period look and is a traditional lobed Roots-type fed by a single SU

88

Production changes to the TC

Changes to the TC during its production were as follows:

26/11 1945 At chassis number TC1850 the headlamp lens design changed from flat glass carrying a horseshoe pattern to a curved glass with a cat's eye pattern.

20/1 1947 At TC2196 the speedometer cable was re-routed to prevent early breakage. Previous cars had suffered from gearbox oil seeping up the cable into the speedometer and the re-routing helped to prevent this as well.

26/8 1947 From TC3414 the voltage regulator was changed to Lucas RF95/2 with exposed fuses rather than the previous Lucas RF91, which had the fuses inside the regulator cover. The original RF91 is now seldom to be seen.

21/10 1947 At TC3856 the carburettors were fitted with hydraulic piston dampers, enabling improved acceleration at low speeds.

8/12 1947 There were major changes to the suspension from TC4251 onwards. 2.5 degree tapered packings were inserted between the front axle and the springs, reducing the caster angle from the original 8 degrees to 5.5 degrees. This was introduced to reduce steering effort and improve directional stability. Whether this was actually noticeable is a moot point.

9/2 1948 From TC4737 the fog lamp fitted became the more modern Lucas SFT462, replacing the previous FT27.

16/3 1948 From TC5039 there was a minor re-design of the steering box drop arm.

14/12 1948 The first TCs specifically designed for export to the United States was introduced at TC7380, carrying the suffix EXU. In fact only 494 of these TC/EXU cars were actually built, the last one being TC10136 on 9 November 1949.

29/11 1949 The last TC, TC10251, left the line.

TC/EXU models did away with these D-lamps fitted next to the rear number plate, replacing them with two Lucas 482-1 lamps mounted high on the end panels of the fuel tank.

Chapter Five

The TD

It was clear to the MG Car Company after the end of the war that the days of the cart-sprung, flexible chassis were over. They secured the services of Alec Issigonis, who was already associated with Alex Moulton and had demonstrated that he and Moulton were in the forefront of suspension design. Before the war the pair had constructed a rubber-sprung single-seat racer, way ahead of its time. Dr Issigonis, as he was then, was commissioned by MG to design the front suspension for a new range of stiff chassis incorporating softer springing. His design of coil spring and wishbone independent front suspension mounted on a subframe first found its way into the MG YA, a four-seater saloon which was first produced in 1947 and used the XPAG engine with a single carburettor. This saloon quickly became very popular, and the front suspension proved a great success, so it was then incorporated in the same chassis – shortened by about five inches – for a new range of MG sports cars to replace the TC from late 1949.

The new sports car was the TD and it went into production in 1950. It is important to note at this stage that the chassis was similar to the chassis of the YB, the later of the two Y-type saloons, the YA having an underslung straight chassis similar to the TC's, albeit being much more substantial, while the YB chassis swept over rather than under the rear axle. This allowed greater suspension travel, desirable in some export markets. The chassis was an immensely strong box-section structure, incorporating the independent front suspension and the live rear axle, with springs considerably softer than those on the TC. Front and rear track were the same as the Y-type's, therefore wider than the TC's, but the wheelbase remained the same at 7ft 10in. The more substantial chassis and redesigned body carried a penalty in that this car was some 2cwt heavier than the TC. It is worth mentioning at this stage that early chassis on the TD were flat without any additional bracing. However, after 100 cars had been produced a tubular steel brace was fitted to stiffen the scuttle. The chassis frame was always painted black.

The TD used the XPAG engine as in the last of the TCs, still with the throw-away oil filter and the earlier distributor, although effectively the engine came straight off the Y-type, incorporating that version's sump, rocker cover, clutch housing, dynamo, starter and engine mountings. The front engine mounting was much more flexible than the TC's. The bearer plate was modified so that the engine was mounted at its centre in a cradle. This meant that the engine would wobble a lot more, had it not been for the fact that a stabiliser bar was fitted between the front of the cylinder head and the mounting attached to the chassis. This is known as the stabiliser bar.

All TD engines were painted deep red. This applied to the cylinder block, cylinder head, and even the sump and timing chain cover. The rocker cover was normally a silver grey-green. The exhaust manifold and clamps were metal

Front and rear views of a production TD. This is a left hand drive example. In comparison with the TC, the first things you notice are the wider wings and the change in wheels from 19-inch wires to much smaller 15-inch steel wheels. But the MG radiator, the folding windscreen, the slab tank and the spare wheel on the tail all remain in place, in the true MG tradition.

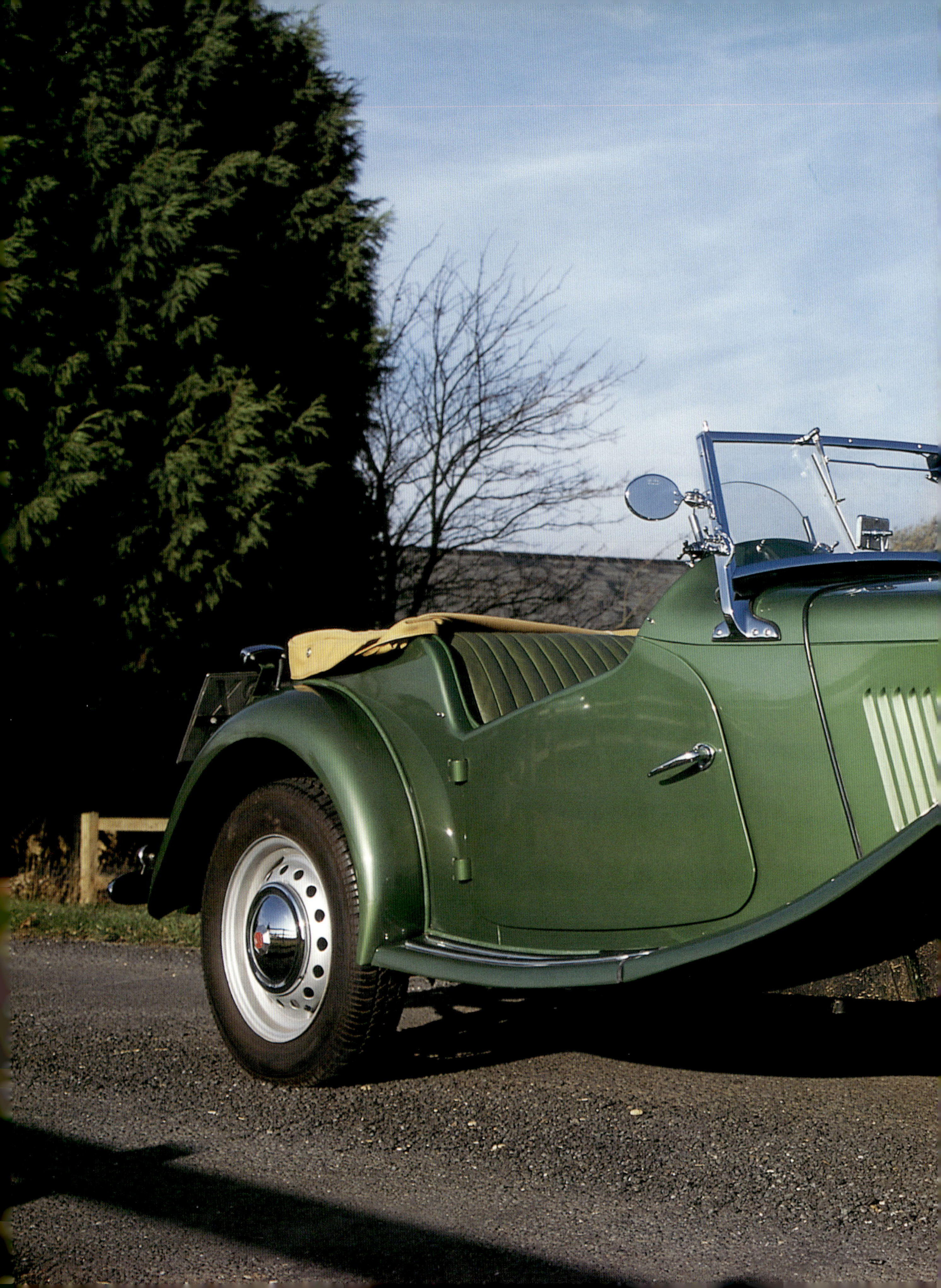

Pat Horsley's very special ex-works TD, one of a run of three prepared by the factory. In effect these were the first TD Mark IIs.

The hood and side screens are as neat as ever.

Opposite: A very special MG. This is TD chassis number 2237, one of three works-prepared cars raced by Dick Jacobs, George Phillips and Ted Lund: among other achievements the team took first, second and third in class at the 1950 TT at Dundrod, and Jacobs won the 1500cc class in the production car race at Silverstone in 1951. Happily, this car is now owned by Dick Jacobs's daughter, Pat Horsley.

sprayed to look like aluminium, the dipstick and the gear lever were chrome plated, and the oil filler cap, gearbox dipstick and engine stabiliser link and hose clamps were cadmium plated. The gearbox remote change housing and the air cleaner manifold were left in natural aluminium. A few cars also appeared with the timing cover, sump and clutch housing unpainted.

The cooling system remained the same, still with an unpressurised radiator, but the dimensions of the radiator differed from those on the TC, so it and the radiator shell are not interchangeable.

The rear axle was a modern hypoid design, derived from other Morris and Wolseley cars of the same era, and came with a 5.125:1 ratio to compensate for the extra weight. The axle had to be split in order to change the crown wheel and pinion, but the consolation to most owners was that the crown wheel and pinion assembly was considerably stronger than those in the TA, TB and TC, and therefore required much less maintenance and attention. The 5.125:1 final drive ratio gave the TD brisker acceleration than the TC but a lower top speed, and owners transferring from the TC found the TD to be somewhat fussier to drive. Many would have opted for the 4.87:1 alternative ratio that was available.

The gearbox also came out of the Y-type, though modified to accept a remote change. Unfortunately this gearbox became the Achilles heel of the car, being its weakest link. Both first and reverse gears are prone to stripping if the car is driven enthusiastically. The TD retained the 7½-inch clutch, at least to begin with, but as will be described later the engine was substantially changed externally during the production run and an 8-inch clutch was fitted along with smaller ring gear. Thus it is important when replacing starter motors to ensure that the pinion teeth of the starter will mesh correctly with the ring gear.

The design of the gears in the gearbox and back axle of the TD (and subsequently the TF) was different from the TA-TC units, the back axle being of the hypoid type needing different shear qualities in its oil, so the previously specified EP140 grade was unsuitable. Instead 90-grade hypoid oil was specified for the back axle and this was recommended for the gearbox as well. Nowadays it is quite safe to use multi-grade gear oils that span the 90-grade rating. The same is also used in the steering racks, so basically a 90-grade gear oil covers all the gear applications in the TD and TF.

The TD used the YB's rack and pinion

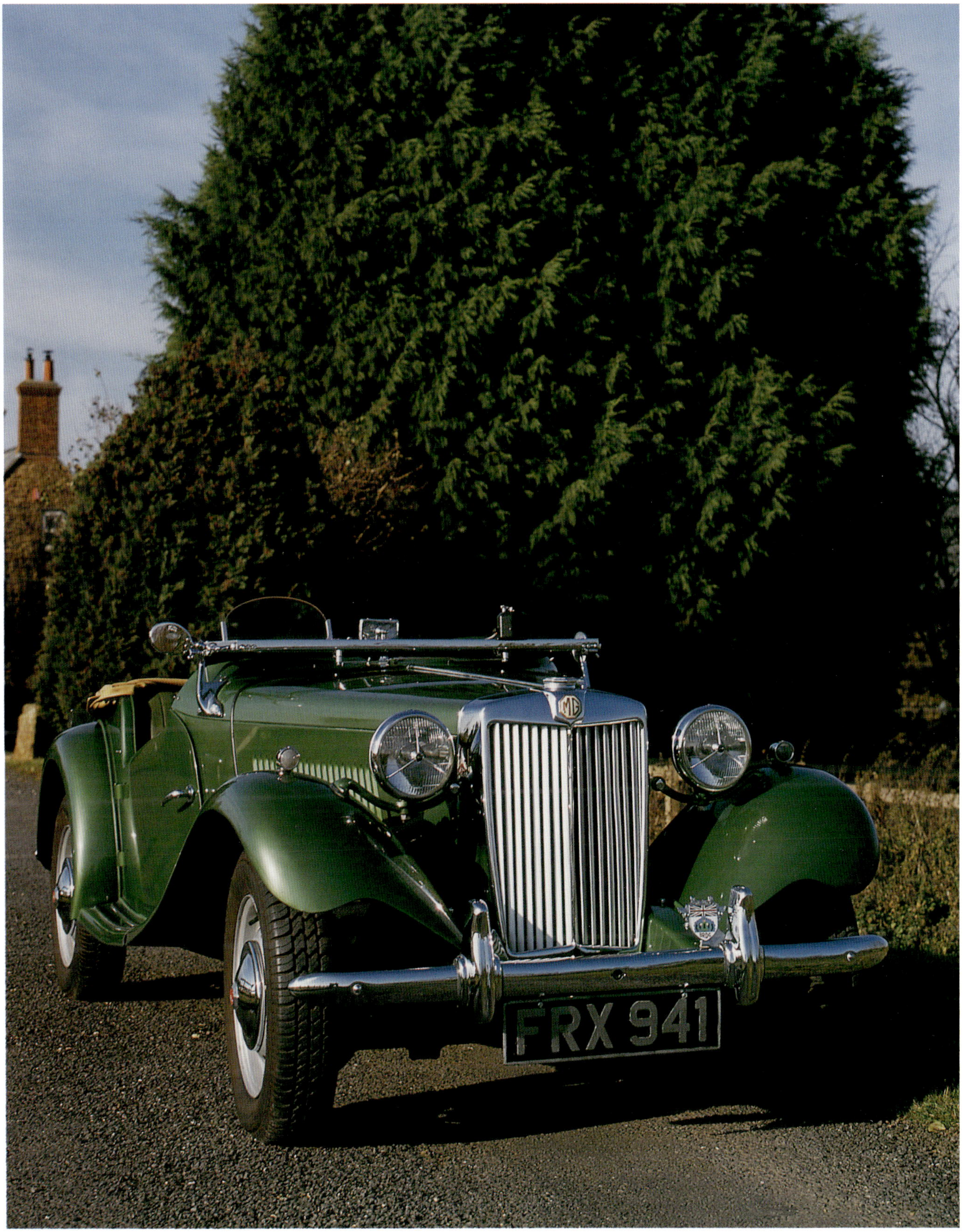
FRX 941

The TD's smaller wheels and sloping tail mark it out from the earlier models, but it is clearly from the same stable.

At the rear, there is now a square number plate and rectangular tail lamps on the wings. This car has a single aeroscreen fitted.

steering, although it is slightly different from the rack fitted to the YB. The rack and pinion steering gives a much more direct, modern feel to the steering, coupled as it is to the independent front suspension. The whole suspension assembly is held on a subframe bolted across the front of the chassis. The steering rack is forward of this subframe, bolted to extensions, and is accessible from under the front of the car It needs fairly regular lubrication and is provided with an oil nipple that faces forward.

The steering column is adjustable fore and aft, with a nut adjusting system similar to the TC's. The steering wheel is of a different appearance, with a more bulbous boss and slender spokes, but the horn push was still situated on the dash panel.

There were now 15-inch disc wheels, fitted with 5.50 section tyres, in place of the TC's 19-inch wire wheels. On the first 250 cars or so the wheels were plain, but they were then replaced by pierced disc wheels, which improved the look of the car.

The brakes were shared with the YB saloon and were Lockheed as before. An important change was to the front brakes, which now had two leading shoes. In this arrangement there are two wheel cylinders per brake, one at the top and one at the bottom, and each of them, when operated, puts an equal pressure on each shoe, so the rear one effectively becomes a leading shoe as well. They are presented square on into the drum, whereas with the arcing action of the earlier single leading shoe system the top of the shoes took the brunt of braking, and therefore wore unevenly and quickly.

The brake drums were of 9-inch diameter with steel drums, but they were of a slightly different design to the TA, TB and TC brake drums. The combined reservoir and master cylinder was still under the floor but of a more modern design. The wheel cylinders at the front are interchangeable but they must be arranged so that the flexible hose is connected to the forward cylinder and the bleed screw to the rear cylinder. The rear brakes operated on the single leading shoe system and the wheel cylinder is at the 9 o'clock position as you look at the back plate. The shoes therefore lie in what you might term a horizontal position. The adjustment method on the TD was different to the TA, TB and TC in that there were "micram" adjusters accessed through the drum with a screwdriver so as to give a very positive adjustment. Provided the cars are used regularly the brakes work well in a balanced manner and can be made to lock up in extremes.

The handbrake on the TD is still of the fly-off type, but is in a different position on the TD, and on the TF, being situated on the propshaft tunnel between the seats. It is pulled up and down rather than to and fro as on the earlier cars. The cables run down the centre of the car, then branch out to the rear brakes. There is no separate adjustment for the handbrake as slack is taken up automatically when adjusting the hydraulic brakes using the micram system.

The major external change was to the car's body. Although initially appearing similar to the TC – in fact the prototype TD had a TC body – it was redesigned for production with different doors and windscreen and, of course, with the smaller wheels, different front wings which swept over the front of the front wheels, and wider rear wings, again with a central rib similar to that of the TC. There was also a rear apron running between the two rear wings into which the bottom of the spare wheel fitted in an indent. There was an extra 4½ inches of width inside body, and slightly more luggage space behind the front seats too, while the less angular lines appeared to make the car look slightly lower than the TC, although this is deceptive as the cars are of almost identical height. For the first time on a T-type, bumpers were fitted front

Offside of the TD Mark II engine, showing the larger carburettors and twin fuel pumps that were standard on this model.

The TD used a pair of Lucas Windtone horns, one each side of the scuttle rather than the previous cars' badge bar mounted items.

Opposite: The TD and the Y-type were featured together in the same brochure.

The Y-type MG in tourer form. The TD derived its independent front suspension, and other components, from the Y-type.

and rear on both home and export cars. The radiator slats were finished in the same colour as the interior trim, though not invariably so, but on the Mark II model described below they were chrome plated.

Paint options offered on the TD were initially the same colours as the TC had been produced in, namely Red, Green, Ivory, Blue or Black, with Red, Green, or Beige trim. There was one slight change in that the Green cars could no longer be had with Green upholstery. Early in 1951 two new colours were added, Autumn Red and Sun Bronze, and if you had an MG Red car you could have Red or Beige trim. Similarly, with Autumn Red or Almond Green you would have Beige trim, with Ivory you could have Red or Green trim, Clipper Blue came with Beige trim, Sun Bronze with Red or Green trim, and Black paint gave you a choice of Red, Green or Beige trim.

This continued more or less through the production of the TD, except that by 1953 the colour choices had been narrowed down to MG Red with Red trim, Woodland Green with Green trim, Ivory with Red or Green trim, Silver Streak Grey with Red trim or Black with Red or Green trim.

As stated, the dynamo and starter came from the Y-type and they are considerably smaller than their TC predecessors. The car inherited the TC's charging systems and at the front the headlights remained free standing as on the TA/B/C but were of a smaller diameter – 7-inch against the earlier car's 8-inch. For the first two years the dipswitch was the same hand-operated one as on the earlier cars,

Introducing the new
TD SERIES
MG
MIDGET
A 'PLUS' version of a world-wide success
HVC 501

The TD had bumpers with overriders fitted as standard. The front wings curve further down over the wheels than on earlier models. Late Mark IIs had a black-on-white radiator badge in place of the traditional brown-on-cream one on this car.

but in 1952 a floor dipswitch was introduced.

There is often confusion about the correct identification of TDs. For example there is the rather confusing TD Mark II. This was basically a competition car with a Stage 2 engine: compression ratio raised to 9.5:1, larger inlet and exhaust valves, twin 1½in carburettors, twin SU fuel pumps and additional Andrex front shock absorbers. These were of the friction type and compensated against excessive roll at competition speeds – the TD's softer suspension meant that it rolled more. These dampers were fitted as an alternative to an anti-roll bar.

The TD Mark II was produced in small numbers from 1950 to 1953. There was no separate engine number to denote the Mark II specification until XPAG17029 arrived, and the engine was then coded XPAG/TD3. However, this is not a safe way to identify a Mark II engine as earlier (at engine number 9408) the TD2 engine, with a larger clutch, etc., had been introduced, coded XPAG/TD2. During this transition period some Mark II engines had the TD2 suffix on the engine but TD3 stamped on the maker's plate. Chassis numbers on the Mark II were identified as TD/C followed by the number. So as it is impossible to identify a Mark II from the

This cutaway from the TD brochure shows the new chassis arching over the rear wheels, and the independent front suspension.

engine, or even the addition of the Andrex shock absorbers or the twin fuel pumps and 1½in carburettors, the one true way to identify this model is to check the chassis number. This will be TD/C followed by the number itself. It was believed early on that the Mark II was fitted with bucket seats, but in fact this was only the early Press cars.

In December 1952 at chassis number TD/C/22613 the Mark II received a slightly new look with a small bulge on the offside bonnet to clear the enlarged air cleaner pipe which had been fitted at about the same time, and a Mark II badge appeared on each side of the bonnet, with a similar badge mounted on the rear bumper. The radiator badges on the TD as on all previous T-types were traditionally brown and cream, but on the Mark II this was changed to black on white. In addition the radiator grille was chromed. Finally a curved handle was mounted on the passenger side of the fascia. These later became known as grab handles.

The TD was a considerably more civilised vehicle than its predecessors and sold in much larger quantities than any previous MG produced. In the years between 1950 and 1953, 30,000 TDs were produced, and it is generally accepted that over 90 per cent were exported. The TD in fact was designed to satisfy those export market needs. There were probably at least seven export versions of the TD and the chassis plate would indicate the market for which the cars were built. Only TDs produced for the home market did not have a market code, and basically home model chassis numbers would be TD12345 and so on.

The TD's running boards had three tread strips.

This type of pierced disc wheel is standard on the TD. Wire wheels only became available to retro-fit to TDs when the TF was in production.

MG T SERIES IN DETAIL

Cockpit of a right hand drive TD. The steering wheel boss is now rounded and the handbrake has moved between the seats, though it is still of the fly-off type.

The production records might indicate an H but this number never appeared actually on the maker's plate.

For export cars, however, the market code was added to the serial number of the chassis. A TD with the number TD12345EXL or EXR would indicate that it was a general export model in either left hand or right hand drive form. Cars so coded could have ended up anywhere in the world. EXR cars would normally have the speedometer calibrated in miles per hour as they were mainly imported to Commonwealth countries, whereas EXL cars would have a speedometer calibrated in kilometres per hour. Occasionally a right hand drive car would be exported to a country operating the metric system, in which case it would have a kph speedometer and the chassis plate would be marked EXR/K. European market cars in left hand drive form had kph speedometers and would be coded EXL/M.

To be pedantic, the first general export TD was TD0332EXR/K built on the 20 September 1949. The first plain EXR was TD0549EXR on January 24 1950, and on 1 March 1950 the first EXL/M was TD0847. Some internal documents would indicate that there were other codes, such as EX/DA for a driveaway chassis with no body, and it is possible that chassis for special TDs such as the Arnolt were coded as TD/EX/DA. Other codes have been identified such as EXE for Eire, EXSA for South Africa and EXM for Mexico. Some New Zealand cars had the code EXN, but their chassis

The rev counter and speedometer are now both in front of the driver, but the central instrument panel is very similar to the TC's. An oil thermometer, a factory option, is fitted to the far right of the dashboard on this car. The steering wheel is radically different from those fitted to the earlier models, with three sprung spokes.

102

plates would only show EXL or EXR.

Cars destined for the United States were differently coded and early ones probably continued with the EXL code, as EXL/M. Some later cars used the code EXU, similar to the TC EXU, and indeed in January 1950 the first TD/EXU appeared as TD0443EXU, but there is no indication whether it was a left or right hand drive car.

Later that year, probably in March, the code for USA cars was changed to EXLU or EXRU. The first EXLU was produced on 20 March as TD1014 and TD1102 was the first EXRU car, originating on 28 March 1950. In 1951 this all changed again, so that cars entering the United States became EXL/NA, which stood for Export Left hand drive, North America. On 18 May 1951 the first of these TDs was TD7781, and this code

A lidded glovebox occupies the left of the dash where the speedometer had previously been.

This car has 7-inch Lucas "Tripod" headlamps. Normal wear was the S700 headlamp with block-pattern lens. The sidelights are the same as on all earlier T-types.

The door trim is very similar to the previous model's.

A sales brochure illustration of a happy couple touring in the United States.

The bucket seats and the registration number FMO 885 tell us that this Mark II TD is one of the 1950 works racing cars.

remained up until the end of production. Nobody seems to know whether there were any EXR/NA cars.

Despite all these various codes there was absolutely no difference in the cars' specifications other than the alterations necessitated by changing from right- to left-hand drive.

The TD service part lists make interesting reading, especially in connection with the factory-offered accessories. For the standard TD these included such things as a badge bar, a Lucas SFT462 fog lamp, a combined oil pressure and water temperature gauge for retrofitting to early TDs, an oil temperature gauge, wider wheels, a luggage rack, a double spare tyre carrier, de-rated Girling shock absorbers, the Andrex friction dampers and alternative rear axle ratios – two of them in fact – of 4.555:1 and 4.875:1.

In addition the Mark II had listed for it special components such as a Lucas 4VRA magneto, flexible oil pipes, a carburettor for fitment with a supercharger, high-compression pistons, sodium-cooled exhaust valves, a revised distributor, a manual ignition advance control, and competition clutch, head gasket and camshafts. None of these were fitted at the factory and they had to be ordered through a dealer.

TDs have of course appeared on wire wheels, but there is no evidence to show that these were available from the factory during production. They are not mentioned in any parts lists, manuals or publicity. What appears to have happened is that when the TF was introduced it was fitted with wire wheels, at which point the factory issued a service bulletin for the TD, listing the wire wheels, half shafts and other items necessary for the conversion. Thus wire wheels did become a factory-approved option, but only from the end of 1953 after production of the TD had ceased.

The early 1950s saw great advances in car design, with the gradual disappearance of the

A TD wearing Zurich plates on the Grimsel Pass in Switzerland, with the Rhone glacier in the background. Standing beside the car is Harry Rummins, Nuffield Service Representative, who was on a visit to the country.

separate chassis. Manufacturers were introducing sports cars that were far more streamlined and modern looking than the TD, and through 1952 and 1953 sales of the TD dropped off as buyers turned to such cars as the Jaguar XK120 and the Triumph TR2. Then in 1953 the Austin-Healey 100 was introduced. This had a devastating effect on the MG Car Company, which had been pressing Lord Nuffield to introduce a more modern MG in the form of the MGA. According to John Thornley, MG's General Manager at the time, the MGA concept had grown out of a series of special vehicles that George Phillips had built up to race at Le Mans. The pre-prototype, coded HMO6, had a TD chassis, the XPAG engine, and a handsome aerodynamic body designed by Syd Enever with a bulge in the bonnet to accommodate the XPAG engine. The car was a bit larger than what turned out to be the MGA two or three years later. It was shown to Leonard Lord, BMC Managing Director, in a vain effort to persuade him that the MGA should be produced in 1953 rather than the TF. Unfortunately, it was three days too late, for in the meantime Donald Healey had made a deal with Lord for the production of the Austin-Healey 100. As a result

The Austin-Healey 100 showed just how outdated the T-type concept had become.

Outdated like the MG but still in production: the Singer Roadster, here working hard for its living in a rally in the early 1950s.

the MGA was put on ice for two years.

The introduction of the Austin-Healey sounded the death knell of the MG T-type. With the introduction of the MGA far off and the TD losing favour both at home and abroad, the MG Car Company faced a difficult few years. Yet the TD, with 30,000 cars sold, was the most successful of all the T-types.

The Arnolt MG TD

In 1952 Nuncio Bertone was a struggling coachbuilder in Italy. He had designed and produced some lovely coupé bodies for Lancia, Borgward and Ferrari before securing a contract with FIAT. By 1952 they deserted him, and he was left with some minor work for Alfa Romeo. Looking for something else to get his teeth into, he saw the TD chassis as a possibility and had two chassis shipped to Italy. Together he and his colleague Franco Scaglione designed and constructed a coupé and a cabriolet and put these on the TD chassis. Quite frankly they were masterpieces, combining English sportiness with Italian flair.

Bertone put the cars on show at that year's Turin Motor Show, more in hope than expectation. His hopes were realised. On the opening day American "Wacky" Arnolt came up ordered 100 of each version, saying he could sell them all in the USA. Thus was Carrozzeria Bertone born again, and the Italian bodybuilding industry moved into a golden age of artistic car bodies that are now classics around the world, from the Alfa Romeo Giulietta to the 250 Ferrari GTO.

The Arnolt MG sold out as "Wacky" Arnolt had predicted. Underneath the body was a standard TD, which in this incarnation really needed a few extra horses, and owners were quick to supply them.

Built by Bertone on TD chassis for Wacky Arnolt in the USA, the Arnolt MG represented the best in European styling of the period.

UMG 400 was based on a TD chassis with a one-off body designed by Syd Enever that later inspired the shape of the MGA.

George Phillips is seen driving UMG 400 at Le Mans in 1951 prior to its retirement with a broken piston.

Production changes to the TD

During the production of the TD many changes were made and a full list of modifications appears as an appendix. The author is indebted to Roger Wilson for this.

To highlight one or two things, during TD production oversized Aerolite pistons were introduced to take the capacity out to 1348cc. Most XPAG blocks could be bored by 0.100in to 1348cc, commonly described as 1350, possibly with an extra 0.10in, but above that there is a danger of the block cracking.

In the writer's experience the last of the XP series of blocks produced, which were the XPAW fitted to the Wolseley 4/44 1954-56, were considerably stronger and could be safely bored to 1370cc without the need to line the bores. The connecting rods were also at the peak of their design at this time and the crankshaft – bearing the latest 168557 code – was infinitely superior to the earlier ones.

The only changes to the XPAW engine needed to make it fit the T-types are changing the sump (which is a completely different shape), blocking the dipstick hole, which on the Wolseley block is at the front offside of the block, and drilling into the blanked off boss on the left-hand side of the block to make a new hole for the dipstick. The front engine mounting plate then needs to be changed.

For fitting the XPAW into a TA, the only additional modification necessary would be changing the mounting brackets for the front engine mounts to the same as those on the TC. Detailed examination will show that the hole in the centre of the mounting bracket for the engine mounting rubbers and bolts is considerably larger on the TC than on the TA.

During the TD production run the XPAG engine received considerable alterations to its specification to make it more "modern".

At engine number XPAG/TD2/9408 an 8in diameter clutch was fitted, necessitating changes to the bell housing. Engines prior to that number have a ⅝in clutch fork shaft. From that number the bell housings have a ¾in clutch fork shaft which is moved back 7mm to accommodate the 8in clutch. The flywheel was also changed to have a larger clutch face. There is a school of thought that at the same time a modified oil pump was fitted, but in fact this did not arrive until engine number XPAG/TD2/14224. This oil pump has an oil filter with a renewable element, and the oil filter housing lies horizontally to the engine, rather than vertically as on the previous XPAGs.

A few engine numbers further on, at XPAG/TD2/14948, a larger 10½-pint finned alloy sump was introduced. This is interchangeable with earlier sumps; the earlier sump was a flat-bottomed one inherited from the Y-Type engine.

At engine number 20942 a cotter bolt fixing for the distributor was introduced in place of the earlier Vernier clamp. At engine number 22735 a modified cylinder head was produced, with round water passage holes. All previous cylinder heads had oval passage water holes and were fitted with ½in reach spark plugs. From this engine number ¾in reach plugs were required. Any head can be fitted to any block, except of course that if you are using a round water passage block with a round water passage head, then the round-holed head gasket should be used. Any other combination requires the oval-holed gasket.

At engine number 24116 a far better camshaft was introduced, incorporating a 5/45/45/5 timing with a 0.327in valve lift and 0.012in rocker clearance. This produced a much more torquey engine which also ran a lot quieter than the earlier unit with 0.019in rocker clearance.

At TD4251 the hub and brake drum assembly was changed. Originally it consisted of a separate drum bolted and riveted to the hub, and now it became a one-piece casting.

A very detailed change was made at TD6035 when the outer front wheel bearing grease retainer, which was a felt washer, was changed to a pressed-on steel cap. This necessitated the hub casting being altered to fit it.

At TD8142 the original RF95/2 voltage regulator, which was a nine-post design, was replaced by the RB106, a five-post unit, and a separate fusebox.

The next modification will interest concours enthusiasts. At TD10751 on left hand drive cars and TD10779 on right hand drive cars, the original chronometric speedometer and rev counter, which had flat dials, were replaced by convex-dial magnetic units. At the same time the on/off panel lighting switch was replaced by a rheostat and the 20-amp ammeter by 30-amp instrument.

There was a detail change the steering rack at TD11111, when the housing for the inner tie rod end was redesigned.

At TD12419 (we are now in December 1951) the nuts securing the spare wheel to its carrier changed from BSF to UNF threads.

At TD13914 the original oil pressure gauge was superseded by a combined oil pressure and water temperature gauge, the first time that water temperature was indicated in the T series.

At TD20374 (LHD) and TD20696 (RHD) the original hood frame, which was a two-bow design, was replaced by a three-bow frame, and the side screens and top covering were modified to suit.

At TD20749 an extra body mounting point was added to each side of the frame adjacent to the tubular scuttle brace mounting.

Originally the rear lamps on the TD were rectangular but at TD21303, towards the end of October 1952, they were replaced by round lamps, mounted on chromed plinths. The rear bumper was modified to suit.

The method of operating the clutch on the TD was very different from the earlier cars. They had a direct linkage between the pedal and the bell housing, whereas the first TDs had a cable-operated linkage pivoted from a boss off the side of the sump which then was connected back to the clutch release rod. From TD22251 the cable was changed to a simpler rod system with a stop bolt added to the pedal bracket on the chassis, so that pedal travel could be limited.

A modification for American cars only, and from TD22315, introduced indicators to these cars. A self-cancelling switch was mounted under the fascia on the driver's side. Obviously this required a new wiring harness, a flasher unit, an override relay for the brake switch, dual-filament bulbs and an indicator lamp on the instrument panel. The only sign of this modification on home market and other cars was that the indicator light hole in the instrument panel was covered by a blank. It wasn't until the TF entered production that indicators became a standard fitment.

There was a somewhat mystifying change to the floorboard design at TD22407 but no one quite knows how the design altered!

At chassis number TD/C/22613 a special trim package was introduced on the Mark II as previously described.

The final recorded modification occurred on 11 March 1953 at TD25973, when a new design of the outer tie rods on the steering was introduced, with improved seals.

Without rhyme or reason there were some changes to the headlamps. On some TDs the headlamps were entirely chrome plated, whereas on others the body is painted black with a chrome rim.

Most TDs were fitted with Luvax Girling shock absorbers similar to those on the TC and fitted with a slightly curved arm, which was connected to the suspension rod via a rubber bush. However, some cars were fitted with Armstrong shock absorbers.

These dampers had a straight arm and were of a totally different design. On most of the Armstrong-equipped cars the front wings were dimpled, as the shock absorbers sat higher up on the chassis and fouled the original wings. There is a rumour also that the engine stabilizer link was modified.

All these design changes could cause considerable complication and maybe controversy in the concours arena: and woe betide a judge who gets it wrong!

TD Driving Impressions

The TD was the first of the T-types and indeed the first of the sports MGs to be fitted with independent front suspension. It also had rack and pinion steering, and the combination of these features made the TD quite a different car to drive from its predecessors.

The TD I drove for this review is a 1950 car, chassis number TD4224, and is therefore fitted with the pierced wheels It is an HXL version, registered CSK814, owned by David Butler. It was originally exported to the United States and when re-imported in 1988 was fitted with a Volvo P1800 engine! The current owner purchased it in 1991, converting it to right-hand drive, and sourced an XPAG engine and gearbox for it. It has the later 8in rod-operated clutch, a centrally mounted windscreen wiper motor and the later type of voltage regulator. The engine is bored out to 1300cc and has a 9:1 compression ratio cylinder head. This has been converted to run on unleaded petrol, is fully gas-flowed and polished, and is fitted with the later and larger TD/TF valves. The 1¼in carburettors and the manifold are all gas-flowed. The exhaust manifold is standard. The engine has been balanced, the flywheel lightened, and a Crane road camshaft fitted.

The back axle ratio has been raised to 4.55:1, which provides a 12.5 per cent increase and gives 17mph per 1000rpm in top. In effect this gearing is similar to the gearing in the TB previously tested, which also produced a 70mph cruising speed at 4000rpm.

The dashboard is standard TD. With a little bit of choke, a tug on the starter instantly sees the engine running and settling down to a smooth idle. The gearbox, unlike that of the TB, had been rebuilt and was very smooth to operate, the new synchromesh on second, third and top gears being especially effective.

My initial impressions were that the TD felt higher off the road than the cart-sprung cars and that the rack and pinion steering gave instant changes of direction. As we headed out into the countryside I became aware that the car would sometimes pitch on rough surfaces, while on particularly rough sections where there was also a steep camber it would – and this is very subjective – feel as if it was likely to fall off the road. However, this was no worse than on the TB I had driven earlier, where bumps tended to throw the car off course. I think the same thing was happening to the TD, but with more refined suspension the effect is slightly different. The trick, I discovered, was to maintain a light grip on the steering and use the throttle to balance it.

The engine pulled very strongly and, as the roads were relatively clear, I was able to give the car its head. It was fully capable at cruising at 4000rpm and revved freely in the intermediate gears up to 5000rpm. The engine also felt particularly torquey, no doubt a characteristic of the Crane camshaft. It accelerated easily from low speeds in fourth gear, so the car could be

Dashboard of David Butler's car is commendably tidy.

David Butler's 1950 TD as driven by the author. Its engine has been enlarged to 1300cc.

driven in a lazy fashion as well as a spirited one. The car was considerably quieter in the cockpit than the earlier models, the improved bulkhead and insulation keeping engine noise away from the driver and passenger.

The brake pedal was much further away than the accelerator and there was quite a lot of travel in the brake pedal before the brakes would come on. Whilst they worked well I would have found it easier had the pedals been more level. The car's owner is somewhat taller than I am and it doubtless suited him perfectly, which is what you do with these cars – you adapt them to suit the individual driver, yet I did feel a slight lack of confidence in the braking system had there been a real emergency.

My final impressions were of a car that had a very nice smooth engine, handled well and held the road well on smooth surfaces, but I was slightly disconcerted by its behaviour on bumpy surfaces, possibly because there was slightly less feedback to the driver than on the cart-sprung TB as to what the suspension was doing.

The seating position was comfortable and it was easy to see that this car could be driven for long distances between stops, as indeed this one has been. It is a frequent visitor to Europe and participated in the 1996 MG Car Club's T Register Continental Tour, which was run to celebrate the 60th anniversary of the TA press cars featured elsewhere in this book. In 1998 it went to Switzerland and in 1999 to Bergerac, followed in 2001by a tour of Brittany and in 2003 Switzerland again to celebrate the 55th anniversary of the Swiss Centre of the MG Car Club.

Shortly after that drive, it was discovered that the rear shock absorbers of the car had deteriorated. This might explain why I felt that the car was behaving strangely on rough surfaces and corners. I arranged another drive the car again and the difference in ride and handling of the car was immediately apparent. Cornering and turn-in inspired confidence and I was able to power the car out of the corners much more easily than before, often with a bit of rear tyre squeal! The pitching I had noted earlier was now completely absent. It was easy to see why contemporary road tests had extolled the superiority of the TD over the TC, as the TD is certainly much easier to drive on the road than the earlier cart-sprung cars. The extra power of the engine obviously helped, as it enabled a degree of throttle steering, although I was still somewhat disconcerted by the pedal positions. David has a fairly loose brake pedal, ensuring that all the brake linings are well clear of the drums, so this was one the reasons for its longer travel.

Chapter Six

The TF

One of the TF press cars, photographed in late 1953.

If the powers-that-be at Abingdon in the mid-1950s had had their way, there would never have been the TF. But as the MGA would not be making an appearance for another two years it was necessary to modernise the TD. During the last year or so of TD production, sales had been falling, as newer and more streamlined sports cars were coming on the scene, so a stopgap had to be found. Happily for MG enthusiasts this resulted in one of the prettiest of all MGs, and certainly the most desirable T-type would be a 1500cc wire-wheeled TF. As so often happens, when it was introduced it was compared unfavourably with its predecessor the TD, especially the Mark II TD, as the engine in the TF was the same as in the Mark II.

The TD had been developed at Abingdon by a team made up of Cecil Cousins, who was

MG's first employee and by then a senior manager, Syd Enever, who went on to design the greatest MG ever built, the MGB, Alex Hounslow, who was a renowned racing mechanic pre-war, and Billy Wilkins. In simple terms what they had done was to take a TC body and put it onto a shortened Y-type chassis; the car was designed properly later. Something similar happened in 1953, when they took matters into their own hands. Cecil Cousins is recorded as saying, "The TF was designed by myself and a couple of other foremen and a tinbasher in a fortnight". They were after a more modern, smoother look, as there were all sorts of pretty cars on the scene like the AC Ace, the Triumph TR2 and the Austin-Healey 100. They got hold of a TD and said, "All we've got to do is lean the radiator back a bit".

Billy Wilkins was a brilliant panel beater and, after hearing the others' ideas for the design of the car, went ahead and made the first set of TF wings. The prototype was built in a fortnight, without a single drawing in sight. The car was then driven to the nearby village of Marcham and back, and left outside General Manager John Thornley's office to await his return from holiday. From that moment the TF was born, although it took six months for the drawing office in Cowley to produce the drawings for mass production.

That first, hand-built TF was made in May 1953 and the car entered production that September. The radiator shell was redesigned and sloped back, lowering the bonnet line, and the radiator itself became pressurised for the first time. The headlamps were faired into the front wings. There was still the chrome-plated folding windscreen frame, but the wipers had been modernised, with a motor underneath the bonnet, the controls in a couple of "glove pockets" on each side of the dashboard, and blades pivoted from the bottom rather than the top of the screen. The system is almost identical with the one on the MG YB. At the back of the

A page from the TF brochure extolling the virtues of the 1250 engine under the bonnet.

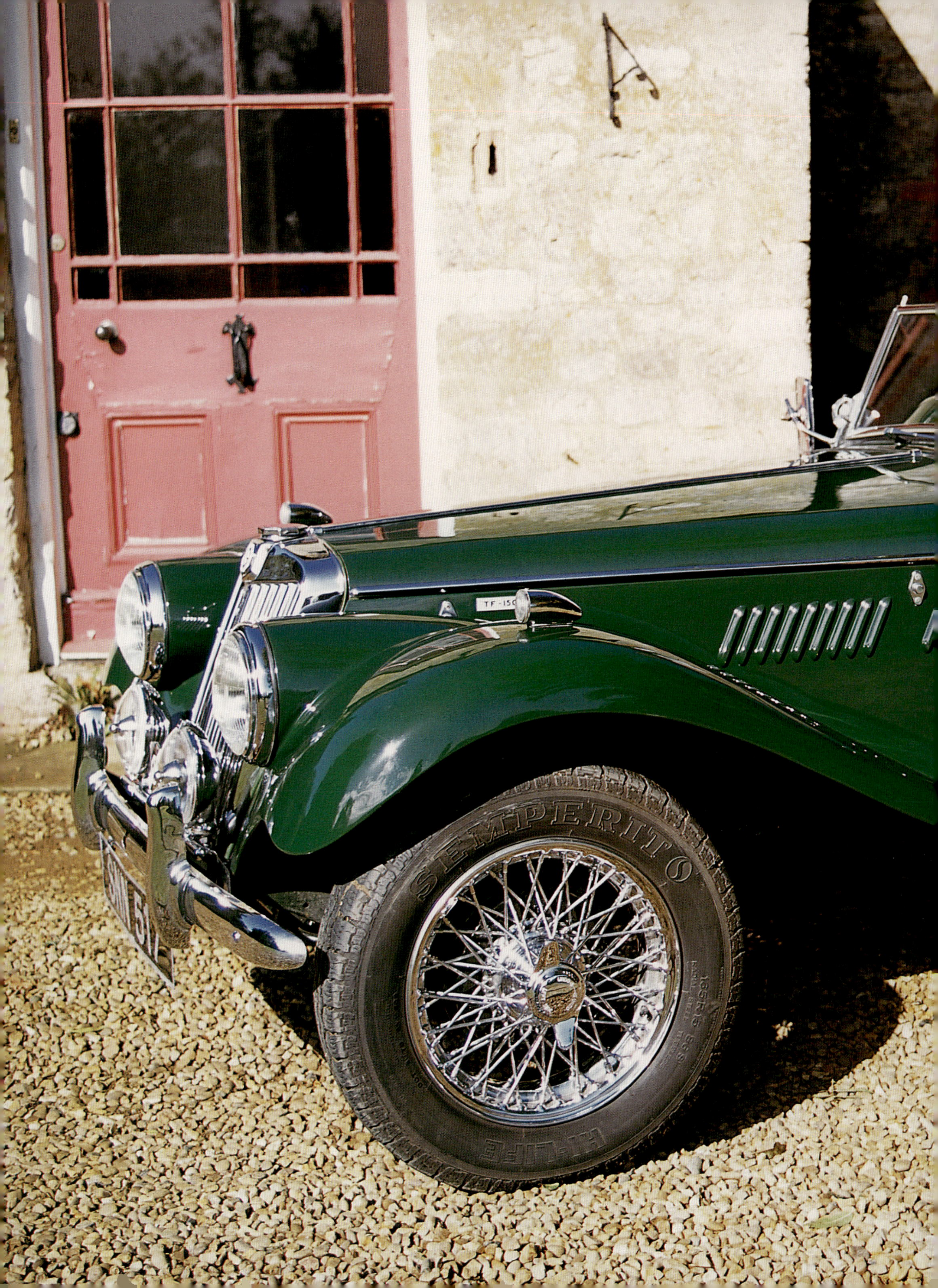
SEMPERITO

Wire wheels were available to order, and left the factory with a silver paint finish. The octagonal radiator cap, for the first time, is a dummy.

Opposite: With weather equipment in place the TF looks very neat.

The mirror dates right back to the first TAs.

car the rake of the fuel tank was increased so that it matched the front radiator in slope and the rather ungainly spare wheel carrier of the TD, was replaced by a more simple structure, akin to the design on the TA/TC cars. The rear lamps were the later TD round ones, and the licence plate lamp was the same as well. However, the licence plate was moved to the centre of the bumper rather than on the driver's side of the spare wheel carrier as on the TD.

The dashboard was completely different from earlier cars. The twin-humped cowl was still there, but it was protected, or rather the driver was protected from it, by a padded vinyl trim. On the central, steeply angled facia panel were, from left to right, an octagonal 100mph speedometer, a matching octagonal dial combining ammeter and water temperature and oil pressure gauges, and – also matching – an octagonal 6000rpm rev counter. The clock was mounted in the speedometer, not the rev counter as on earlier models. Immediately above the central dial were three warning lamps: blue for the indicators, green for the ignition and red for low fuel level, the allotted colours being a bit contrary to accepted practice. To the right of the rev counter is the starter pull knob and up above the rev counter is an auxiliary switch which could be wired to operate the optional fog lamp. To the left of the speedometer is the choke and to its right is the lights switch, which is entirely different from the TA-TD unit. A first pull gives sidelights, then a twist to the right and a second pull turns on the headlights. The switch for the panel lamps worked similarly, and the twist and second pull would switch on the map reading lamps, which were mounted under the cowl in front of each passenger. The ignition switch was to the lower left of the rev counter. The horn button also moved, but still not to the steering wheel boss. It was fitted under the right-hand cowl at the 2 o'clock position relative to the steering wheel. The turn indicator the switch was below it. For the first time there was provision for fitting a radio, in the nearside glovebox.

While earlier T-types had a one-piece backrest for both seats, on the TF this arrangement was replaced by generously upholstered individual bucket seats with hinged backs. There was a slight increase in luggage space behind them.

The chassis is identical to the TD in appearance, with the rear springs of the same number and thickness of leaves, but the camber was reduced by 1¼in as the TF's weight bias was more towards the front. The transmission and back axle were the same, except that the back axle ratio became the one carried over from the TD Mark II, at 4.875:1.

The XPAG engine was nearing the end of its production and had become slightly more sophisticated, but the one in the TF was essentially the XPAG/TD3 unit used in the later examples of the TD Mark II. The cylinder head was completely Mark II, with large valves, stronger valve springs and an 8.1:1 compression ratio. It was also fitted with twin 1¼in SU H4 carburettors but they had a shorter body mounting than those on the TD Mark II and, as a matter of detail, the dashpots were vented slightly differently. The fairing of the wings into the bonnet had a negative impact on accessibility for the DIY mechanic, the bonnet sides now being fixed, and because the bonnet line was lower the original oil-bath air cleaner was dispensed with and individual Vokes "pancake" air cleaners were fitted. The TF had the same distributor as the TD Mark II and some of the very last of the TDs, this being the 40367 unit mentioned earlier.

In this form the engine produced 57bhp, which was not really very much more than the 55bhp of the TC, while in early road tests the car was found to be somewhat slower than the Mark II TD. As usually happens when a new MG is introduced, it took a long time for enthusiasts to accept the TF. There was considerable

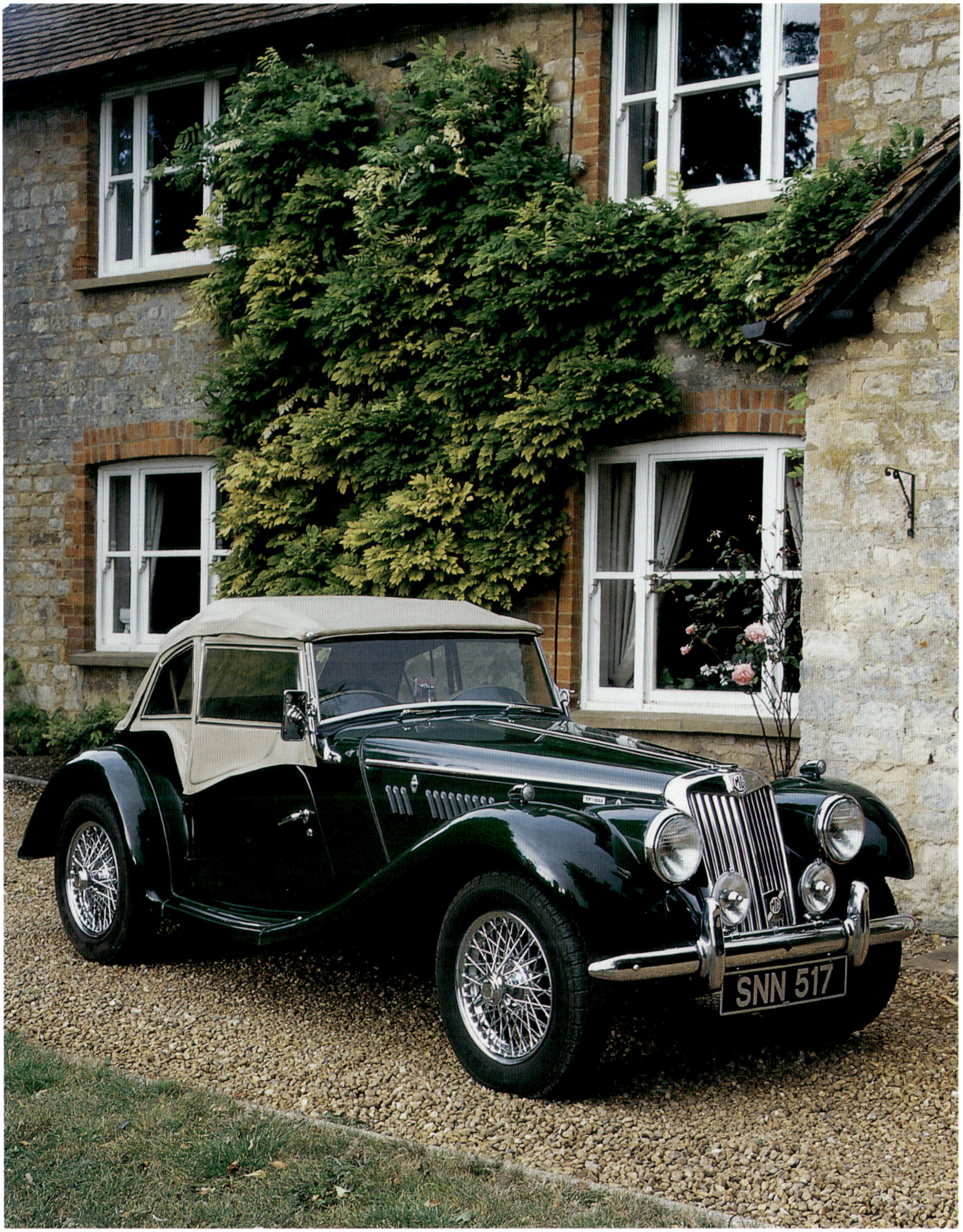
SNN 517

MG T SERIES IN DETAIL

The rake of the radiator grille can be seen, and the bonnet line is lower than before. The windscreen is also more raked than the TD's.

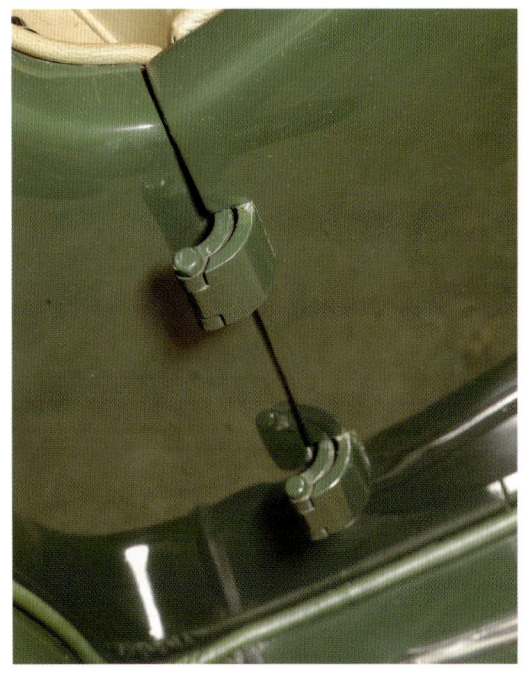

The door hinges are still external, but are stronger and curved.

disappointment in its performance and questions were asked as to why it did not have the new 60bhp 1500cc BMC B-series engine installed in the new MG ZA saloon that had come out at the same time.

This particular XPAG block was, however, susceptible to overboring and could, if carefully done, be taken out to 0.120in oversize. This conversion was offered by aftermarket tuners and subsequently became the standard for T-types in competition.

This was the golden age of special building, and the XPAG engine had found its way into a wide range of cars offered by different manufacturers, such as Lotus, Cooper and many others. Their builders had experimented with enlarging the XPAG engine to 1500cc by boring it right out and lining it back to 72mm, giving a capacity of 1466 cc. This gave the engine a useful power increase but made it very unreliable: the top deck could collapse unless strengthened by

The sleeker, lower lines of the TF are evident here, along with the faired-in headlamps. This is Paul Plummer's TF 1500, chassis number TF 8918, built in January 1955 and registered in March.

The familiar double-humped scuttle is still there, but the top edge is padded and covered in leathercloth. On the TF the number plate is rectangular and sits above the bumper.

means of a rod stuffed up through the centre main bearing to prop it up! Obviously this was not satisfactory for the purposes of the MG Car Company, so the factory embarked on developing its own 1466cc version of the XPAG in response to the call for more power. They altered the layout of the bores so that the front and rear pairs were siamesed, with no water space between cylinders one and two or between numbers three and four. By adopting this method they were able to retain the existing bore centre spacing. Larger pistons were required, and at the same time the connecting rods were strengthened, their thickness being increased very slightly. The compression ratio was raised to 8.3:1, and the new XPEG engine produced 63-64bhp with a useful increase in torque.

The model name was then changed to TF1500, the only sign being the addition of TF1500 badges on the bonnet sides. Eventually 3400 TF1500s were produced against 6200 1250cc cars. You will conclude from this that the total production of TFs between 1953 and 1955 amounted to 9600. While the TF was in production it failed to draw much praise from the motoring press. It wasn't until the MGA had been in production for a few years that the beauty and worth of the TF came to be appreciated, and now of course it is the most expensive T-type to buy.

The very first TFs had the fuel pump on the bulkhead, using the low-pressure system inherited from the TA, TB, TC and TD, but early in production this was deleted and replaced by a high-pressure AUA54 pump mounted low down

Cockpit of the TF. Immediately obvious are the individual bucket seats and the completely new dashboard layout with open gloveboxes on both sides.

on the chassis near the fuel tank. It was therefore a pusher rather than a puller, which the previous AUA25 fuel pump had been.

The relay for the turn indicators, the voltage regulator, starter switch, fuse block and so forth were mounted in exactly the same way as they were on the TD but the Lucas Windtone horns were now mounted low down under the radiator, just below the steering rack.

As a result of the lower bonnet line and the smaller radiator grille, the radiator itself was different from its predecessors and the system was pressurised. The pressure cap was located under the bonnet and the octagonal cap on the top of the radiator grille is a dummy. There was a revised water outlet between the head and the header tank and this enabled a more modern thermostat to be fitted.

The chassis numbering of TFs is also different from that of previous T-types. Instead of utilising the Abingdon factory's telephone number, 251, for the first production TF, it was in fact 501, being numbered HDA13/0501. The two prototype TFs were numbered TF0251 and TF0250, which was most unusual, as you would expect them to be 251 and 252. TF0250 was the car built on 12 May 1953 and was fitted with a

The TF has larger, curved door handles.

TD Mark II engine, XPAG/TD3/26849. This was probably the car left outside John Thornley's office.

Three months elapsed before TF0251 was completed on 8 August, and this had the standard TD engine in it, albeit one of the later ones, XPAG/TD2/29748. Although for a long time these cars remained in obscurity it is now believed that both prototypes have been located and are in private ownership.

To further complicate matters, the chassis numbering for TFs incorporated a new standard coding system introduced throughout the new British Motor Corporation. This was very different from the earlier and more simple MG numbering systems. For instance from the chassis number HDP36, the "HD" would tell you that the car was a TF Midget two-seater; "P" would indicate the paint colour: A denoted Black, B Light Grey, C Dark Red, E Mid Green and P Ivory. The first numeral following these letters would be 1 for home market right hand drive, 2 for general export right hand drive, 3 for general export left hand drive, and 4 for North America left hand drive. The second number would indicate the type of paint used on the car, which in the case of the TF would be 3 for cellulose, 5 for primed and 6 for cellulose body with synthetic wings. The last two numbers are the serial number of the chassis. As on all previous MGs the chassis number is stamped on the left front frame extension where it is preceded with the initials TF. The identification plate doesn't carry the TF prefix.

There is no distinguishing the chassis numbers between TF1250 and TF1500 and you have to look at the engine for this, as the 1250 is coded XPAG/TF whereas the 1500 is coded XPEG followed by the engine number.

Cars that went abroad would often carry the code CKD, which stood for Completely Knocked Down, in that the cars were exported in bits to be assembled at their point of destination. This was commonplace in exports to South Africa, Australasia and the Far East.

By the time the TF was produced there was

The new instrument panel features three octagonal dials. It is tucked under the scuttle rather than being flush with it, and is steeply angled. A Bluemels steering wheel has been fitted to this car - the standard wheel is the same as on the TD.

Passenger side glovebox, with wiper knob visible.

very little to distinguish between cars built for the home market and overseas markets, especially the North America. One of the reasons for this was that the TF dashboard was suitable for either left or right hand drive. As a result of this, factory stocks of spares could be rationalised and reduced, although obviously for items such as steering racks both left and right hand racks had to be kept in stock. Similarly, several different types of light units had to be stocked due to varying dipping regulations around the world.

Although the T-types had gone through many years of development and refinement since the introduction of the TA back in 1936, and the TF was to be the last of the line, there were nonetheless several modifications to the car during its production run, the first being the aforementioned change of fuel pump, which occurred on TF1501 and for which the wiring loom had to be altered as well.

At TF3495 the carburettor dashpots were adapted to incorporate piston dampers, retarding piston movement when the throttle was opened suddenly. This helped provide a slightly richer mixture. When this modification was announced it was retro-fittable to all TFs, and it is now very difficult to find a non-damped set of TF carburettors.

There was a minor improvement to the front hub grease retainers on wire-wheeled cars at TF3811, and from TF4760, on all right hand drive cars, the threads on the tie rod and the ball studs were changed from BSF to UNF. The grease fittings on the track rod ends were also changed, but strangely the threads on the track rod and in the bores of the track rod ends remained BSF. The left hand drive cars weren't altered until TF4910, approximately one month later in April 1954.

TF6501 was the first TF1500 and, apart from

There was more space around the pedals than before, as on the later TD.

MG T SERIES IN DETAIL

Transverse and longitudinal sections of the XPAG engine in the TF.

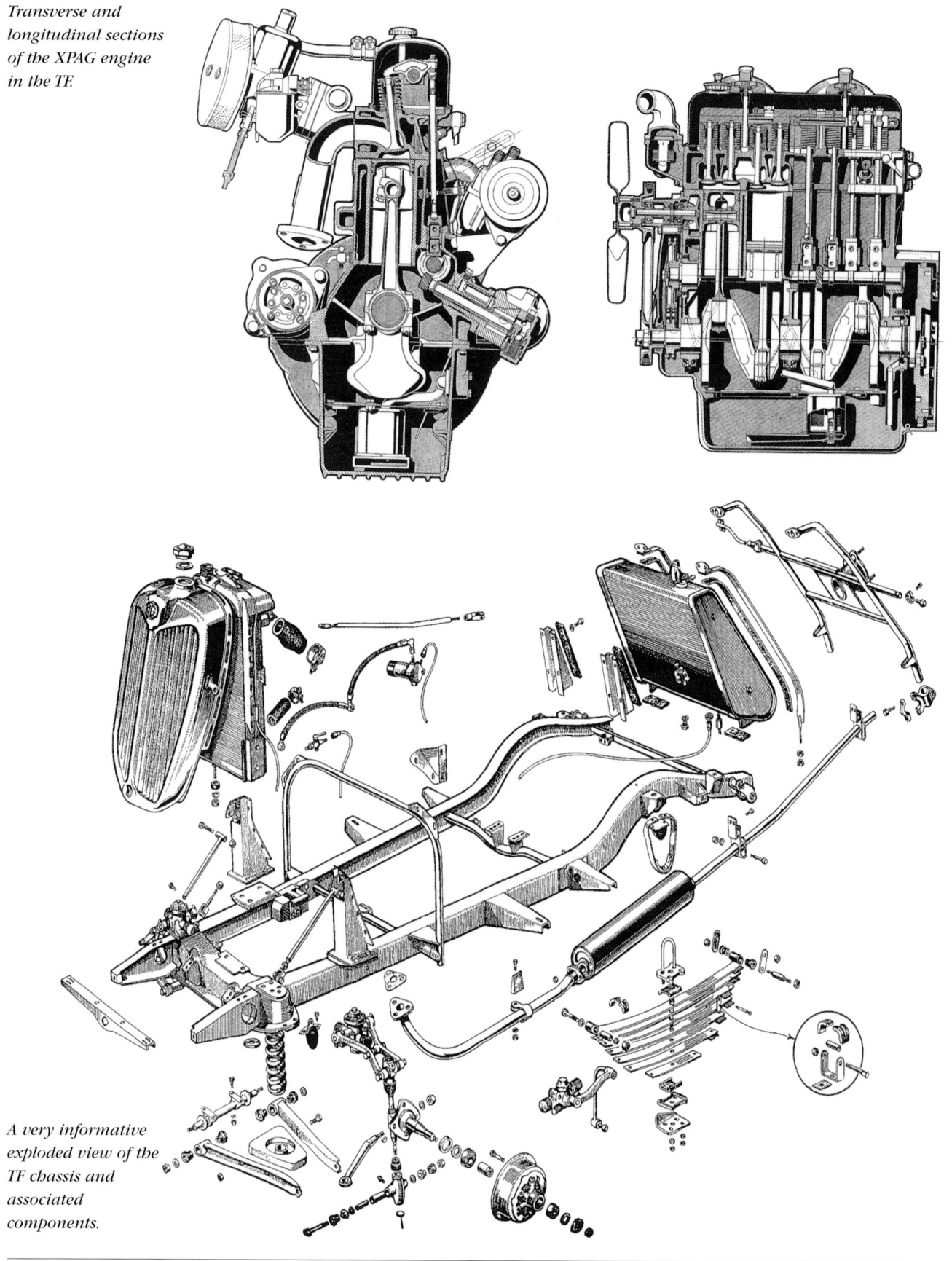

A very informative exploded view of the TF chassis and associated components.

THE TF

the obvious, reflectors were added to the back of the body. From TF6651 to 6750 the engine type was varied back to the 1250cc XPAG/TF. The 1500 then accounted for TF6751 to 6850, a further run of 1500 XPEG engines having been produced. In terms of days this run of 100 cars actually occupied two days of production, 24 and 25 August 1954!

At TF6887, which was a wire-wheeled car, the wheels were changed. The early type had a shallow dished inner flange, whereas the later ones had a deeper dished flange. The wheel size and number of spokes remained unchanged at 4Jx15 and 48 respectively.

The last 1250-engined car was TF6950, and from TF6951 only the XPEG engine was fitted. The last car was produced on 4 April 1955 at TF10100. For nit-picking concours enthusiasts, at TF8146 the design of the cast portion of the horns changed slightly, but the number given to

This shows how the rev counter drive cable and reduction gearbox are fitted to all XPAG engines and to the MPJG as well

Nearside of the engine. The new pressurised radiator can be seen. The alloy rocker cover is from the run of XPAG engines fitted to the TC in 1946.

MG T SERIES IN DETAIL

THE TF

Opposite: The TF's bonnet sides were fixed, limiting access to the engine. It is cramped in there, and replacing a core plug, for example, would be a nightmare. The pancake air filters are standard.

The TF1500 engine gets a plug in the sales brochure.

The TF 1500 badges on either side of the bonnet are the only means of identification of this larger-engined model.

it by Lucas, WT614, remained unchanged.

As noted above, there were five colour choices for the body of TF, and each of them had their own upholstery matches. Black cars could come with either Red, Green or Biscuit upholstery, the MG Red with Red or Biscuit, the Almond Green with Green or Biscuit, the Ivory with Red or Green, and Birch Grey with Red upholstery. The colours of the interior and the chassis and engine were all standardised.

The seat coverings initially look like leather but in fact are a combination of leather and leathercloth. They were assembled so that the front of the squab, the top of the cushion and the side panels of the cushion were leather and the rest of the covering leathercloth, as was the rest of the interior trim, apart from the top edges of the map pockets, which were leather. Carpeting was always black on top of a rubberised felt "underlay" and was secured by lift-the-dot fasteners. The firewall and transmission tunnel were covered with carpet, but behind the seats the luggage compartment was not. The TF dashboard was painted metal, somewhat more utilitarian than the predecessors. An accepted opinion is that was painted the same colour as the car's interior, with the metal instrument panel a sort of bronze colour, edging towards light tan. It had a chromium bead running round its edge. As before, the underdash area was closed in by a fibreboard panel that protected passengers from the wiring, but as happened on all previous T-types these usually warped and were discarded quite early on when the owner wished to get at the back of the dashboard to interfere with the wiring. The hood and side screens were tan, either in double duck or canvas, and the metal frame was a matching colour. The tonneau cover which came with the

A British competitor in a TF on a snowy Umbrail Pass in the 1954 Alpine Rally.

A drawing illustrating the increased cylinder bore of the TF 1500 XPEG engine compared with the 1250 XPAG version, and the siamesing of the pairs of cylinders that was necessary to accommodate it.

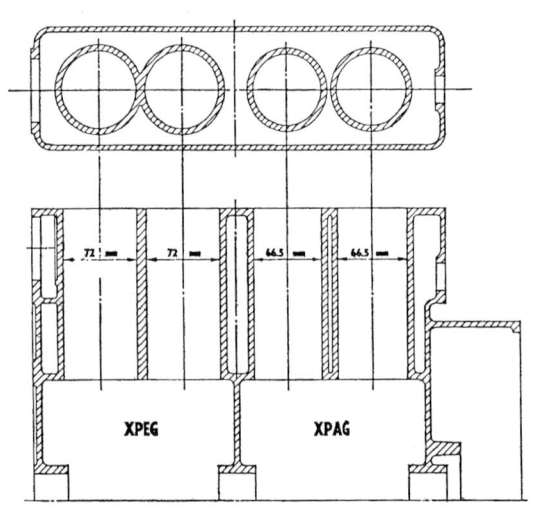

car was only a half tonneau covering the area behind the seats, usually of a tan canvas material but occasionally black vinyl.

As before, the chassis was painted black. You will find that the Armstrong shock absorbers were usually left unpainted in aluminium, but the arm itself was painted black as were the gearbox and propshaft covers. When the cars came out of the factory and all the brake pipes had been fitted, the whole lot was painted black, but there are lot of brass, copper and aluminium parts attached to the chassis which, given the opportunity, are left unpainted by rebuilders and restorers.

The engine was the nice dark red colour adopted by the MG Car Company in 1948. The exhaust manifold was not painted as it gets too hot, but was aluminium sprayed. These days it can be finished with very high temperature spray paint, which can be obtained in various lurid colours if you are so inclined! One can easily get carried away with detail, and a lot of the small parts on the engines were usually painted deep red, but every now and again black ones would turn up, as the Morris engine plant in Cowley, where the engines were produced, probably didn't have as dedicated a workforce as Abingdon, and you might find engines whose small parts are some red, some black, all black, all red, etc. The only part left unpainted was the gearbox remote control housing, all the other aluminium parts being originally painted red, including the bell housing, but these days most of the aluminium items on the engines are left unpainted. Most of the drain plugs, oil lines, priming plugs, etc., together with any other copper and brass parts, were usually left unpainted, but occasionally would have appeared red. Various other items were cadmium plated, such as the gearbox dipstick and the oil filler cap, but the engine dipstick and the gear lever were chromium plated.

There were some optional extras, which can be found listed in the TF Service Parts List, and items including wire wheels, Andrex friction shock absorbers and alternative axle ratios of 4.555:1 and 5.125:1 were available. There was also a

A wire-wheeled left hand drive TF, complete with boot rack, shot for the American market.

This left hand drive TF, wearing Michelin X radial tyres, was shot in Genoa.

MG T SERIES IN DETAIL

A left-hooker TF racing at Sebring in Florida in 1955. The Morgan ahead narrowly avoided a pile-up when the Porsche span out on the corner.

The identification plate on Paul Plummer's TF. Decoded, HDE 13 means HD for MG, E for mid-green, 1 for home market and 3 for cellulose paint. XPEG denotes the 1500 engine. The independent front suspension was common to TD and TF, along with rack-and-pinion steering. The anti-roll bar is a later addition.

luggage carrier, an external rear view mirror, a badge bar and a full-length tonneau cover.

In 1954 the company printed a successor to an earlier special tuning guide, and this will be referred to in the chapter on Competition Cars, but the extra equipment available for the TF included high compression pistons, a magneto ignition system, different distributors, a competition clutch and two alternative camshafts, the AEG122, which can be described these days as a modest rally-type road cam, and another camshaft coded 168551 which was intended for racing and indeed gave a considerable boost in power, though at the time it was not recommended for road use as an engine fitted with it wouldn't idle evenly below 1500-2000rpm.

These days even this camshaft could be regarded as perhaps no more than a fast road/race cam, and if the engine is balanced it can be made to idle at 1000rpm quite comfortably.

As with TCs and TDs there was quite a large aftermarket industry in place, from dealers such as Thompson's and Derrington's, and in the United States several different manufacturers offered additional bits and pieces, including the Judson supercharger specially adapted to fit under the TF bonnet.

Meanwhile, out in the marketplace, the TF, pretty and nimble as it was, was being jostled by almost a host of more up-to-date sports cars. The 2.6-litre Austin-Healey 100 could comfortably exceed 100mph and the Triumph TR2, announced the same year as the TF, could do much the same with its 2-litre 90bhp engine. If fitted with the optional overdive it could cruise all day at speeds well in excess of the TF's maximum. Both these cars in particular represented a new generation, in styling and performance, that left the MG trailing far behind. The ancient Yorkshire firm of Jowett had its distinctly modern and attractive 2-seater Jupiter with flat-four engine, which drove and handled well. Buyers with more money could choose the delicious AC Ace, and for really fast motoring the Jaguar XK was an obvious candidate – and at a compelling

Denis Hulme, later to achieve considerable fame as a racing driver, at the wheel of a TF in his first competitive event.

No change in the style of door trim, and the door latch is the same as on all other T-types.

The twin bucket seats fold forward for better access to the luggage area.

price. As for more traditional sports cars, the Singer marque was still around, and offered a 1500 Roadster, but it was a four-seater and a good deal more staid than the pre-war Singers. Morgan was successfully selling its 2-litre Plus Four, with power outputs up to 90bhp and acceleration to match, which would have had a direct appeal to the T-type fancier.

Something else happening, though, during the time of the TD and TF was MG's increased interest in record-breaking, and one of the engines installed in the MG record breaker at the time was a very highly developed XPAG, bored out to 1517cc, which with the benefit of a supercharger and the addition of nitro-methane in the fuel produced 231bhp at 6700rpm. George Eyston used the car with supercharged and un-supercharged engines and he and Ken Miles, using the unblown engine, took several class records including running at 120.74mph for 12 hours. With the sprint engine, again unblown, which at the high altitude of the salt flats produced no more than 84bhp, a flying mile was covered at 153.69mph.

Driving impressions

I drove this particular TF several years ago in mid-Wales during a weekend gathering I had organised. Initially I found the car's seating position rather high, but this is subjective, as is the feeling that this model is a bit bulbous. To explain, the top rail of the windscreen was lower in relation to my eyes than the screens that I had sat behind in previously tested T-types and the lower bonnet line further adds to the effect. The bulbous feeling disappears very quickly once you are seated in the car and there is considerably more space in the cockpit for both driver and passenger. The bucket seats take the credit for this as they occupy less space and also give more room in the luggage area behind the seats. It is thus possible to reach back between the seats to remove a small thing such as a vacuum flask while travelling along.

The dashboard is spacious as well, with glove boxes each side for storing small items as long as these are kept clear of the windscreen wiper knobs that protrude into the tops of the glove boxes. This set-up is very different from the TD and earlier models, as the wiper motor is now under the bonnet and drives the dash mounted wipers with a rack and pinion system, very much in the way all modern cars do now. This and, for example, the sealed-beam headlamps set into the wings, demonstrate the march of progress.

As was the case on all the T-types I drove, this one started instantly, with a little choke, and settled down into a smooth idle. The engine in this car is a standard 1250cc unit with the standard inlet and exhaust manifolds and twin 1½-inch SU carburettors. It took me a while to get used to the main instruments being in the centre of the dashboard, with oil pressure and water temperature indicated on separate instruments between the speedometer and rev counter. The gearbox was easy to use and the 8-inch clutch relatively light in operation. There also appeared to be slightly more room around foot pedals and the brake pedal was more level with the accelerator and clutch than on the TD, making it easier to brake and quickly hit the accelerator again or vice versa, and even to heel and toe.

The suspension was firm but comfortable and as we made our way down the single-track road to the main A470 the car turned neatly into the tight corners and felt very controllable on the steep descents. It was a fine sunny day so no side screens were fitted, although the car carried very efficient weather-proofing, with a well-fitting hood and side screens if necessary.

Turning onto the A470 and heading off towards Llanidloes the car accelerated briskly but it was noticeable that the standard TF engine ran out of puff quite early and that it had much less power in reserve for overtaking than the 1500cc version or tuned 1350cc

Below: As on the TD, the handbrake was between the seats, though still of the fly-off type.

Bottom: The starting handle is clipped in the luggage compartment.. On earlier cars it was fitted on the board behind the seats.

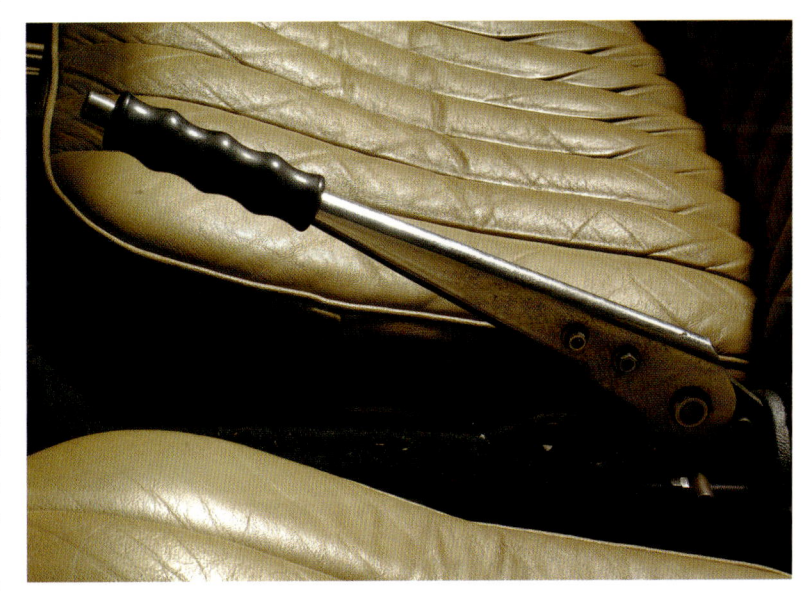

engines in the TB, TC and TD cars that I had previously tested. Nevertheless the TF cruised comfortably at 55-60mph and its brakes were equally good, pulling the speed down without any drama for the sharp left turn into the service road which feeds into Llanidloes now that the town has been bypassed.

Our road then climbed steeply out of the town and the TF, whilst not exactly struggling, did not leap up this hill as friskily as the other T-types I had driven, but it was very competent and made a nice drum from its exhaust as the road ran between high hedges to the summit. Going down the other side involved a series of fast, sweeping left and right handers and the TF behaved impeccably here, turning into and powering out of these corners without the need to brake. Speed was then increased on a long-ish straight, at the end of which the road plunged steeply down to the valley floor, calling for heavy braking to make an almost 90-degree turn over a bridge. The brakes were well up to this job and the car was unruffled by the tight turn.

Now came a very steep climb where it was important to stay committed. With foot hard down, hoping nothing was coming the other way and praying there would be no cows dozing in the road, we roared to the top! All was well, and we splashed on through the puddles to our destination, the car riding easily over the bumpy surface which, for instance in the TB I used to own, was indeed a rough ride.

There was no noticeable whine from the gearbox or the back axle and the brakes were reliable and fade-free despite some consistent hard work in this hilly terrain. The rigidity of the chassis and the body was such that there was no worry about the doors opening unexpectedly as happens with the TA/TB/TC once the bodies start to loosen a bit. The engine in the car was a 1250 XPAG to TF specification, running the most recent spec crankshaft, and the camshaft fitted was the standard late TD/TF camshaft also used in the Wolseley 4/44 with its 5/45/45/5 timing and 8mm valve lift. This is the same camshaft as was fitted to my TB and in my view is the best camshaft to fit to any XPAG engine in any state of tune if the car is used solely for road work.

Were money to be no object a TF would figure very strongly, in my opinion, as the best of the T-types for practical usage. The only downside, as has been noted elsewhere, is the lack of access to the engine, and although access hatches are provided, retiming the distributor, replacing the oil filter and repairing core plugs are difficult jobs. It is best to be patient and accept the chore of removing whichever front wing is getting in the way. Other than that, considerable pleasure can be had from driving these models – not more fun than in a TB for instance, just fun of a different nature – and fun is what you get from driving any of the T-types. As the driver of one of the latest MG ZR hatchbacks, I can assure you that the element of fun is still there!

A contemporary advertisement showing accessories available for the TF from Motor Glaziers Ltd of Birmingham.

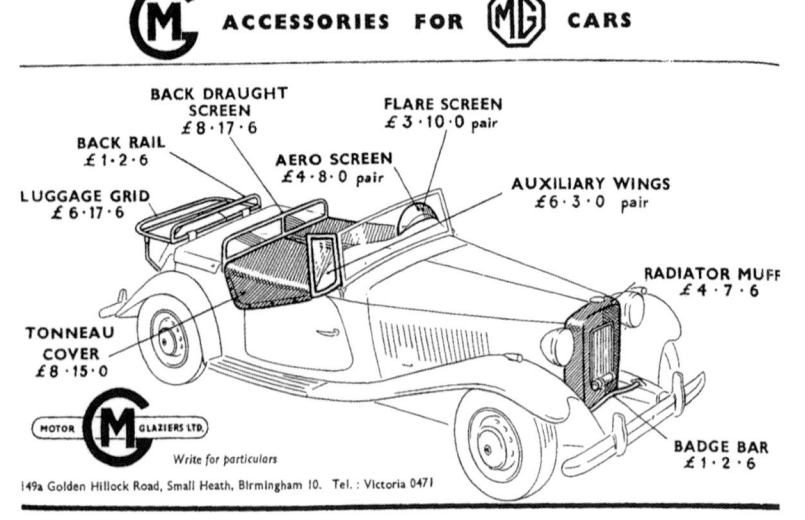

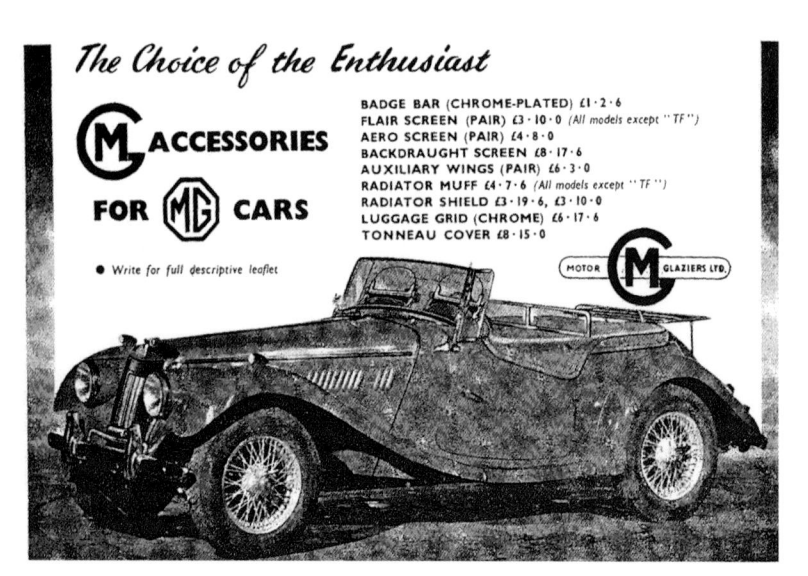

THE TF

In addition to the Austin-Healey 100, the TF was up against the Triumph TR2 in the market place. The TR2 ahead of a Cunningham and a Panhard in this shot at Le Mans in 1954 took 15th place and averaged an amazing 34.6mpg.

Chapter Seven

Racing T-types

Alan Tomlinson with his TA at the 1939 Australian Grand Prix, which he won.

The MG two-seater was always a car suitable for racing, and the launch of the TA must have been greeted with eager anticipation by drivers in the mid-1930s who had been racing earlier MGs. Yet they were disappointed by the TA, as its MPJG engine was distinctly uncompetitive and not amenable to any degree of tuning beyond "blueprinting" and optimum ignition and carburettor settings. A few TAs did take to the track, however, one being raced at Brooklands by the Haselbonck brothers. It is even more remarkable that Alan Tomlinson and others got a TA to go so well in Australia that it won the Australian Grand Prix in 1939. One has to study its specifications to understand how it managed to do this.

The successes in 1936 of the factory-sponsored trials teams, the Cream Crackers in MG Midgets and The Musketeers in Magnettes, led the company to build new trials cars based on the TA for both teams for 1937. The cars had cycle wings, off-road tyres and two spare wheels, the Cream Cracker cars being finished in cream with brown wings, the Musketeer cars all red. At the end of the 1937 season the Cream Crackers again carried off the MCC Team Championship, as they had in 1936.

At Donington Park in 1937 three TAs were entered in a 12-hour race organised by the Derby and District MC. Three of the Cream Cracker cars were entered, driven by Archie Langley and Johnny " Jesus" Jones, Jack Bastock/Ken Crawford, and Ken MacDermid/Maurice Toulmin. The TAs ran more or less faultlessly and won the Team Prize, beating the fancied Rileys and Austins, both makes having much greater racing experience at that time, though not the team management experience that John Thornley brought to this one-off race! For 1938 the Musketeer cars were fitted with superchargers and the Cream Crackers got the 1548cc engine from the MG VA saloon, but this did not seem to be enough and the engines were bored out to 1707cc. Thus equipped, the Cream Crackers won the championship for a third time.

Yet it was not until the XPAG engine appeared in the TB that a potential was seen for seriously racing a T-type. The onset of the Second World War stopped all thought of that, so it was not until the late 1940s that T-types – this time TCs – began to be seen on the tracks in any numbers. During this period a lot of talented engineer/drivers were finding their way into motor sport, with the growth of the 750 Motor Club nurturing several of them as car and engine designers. Men such as Colin Chapman, John Tojeiro, John Cooper, Jim Leonard, Brian Lister and Harry Lester were either arriving on the scene for the first time or re-emerging after war service. They all saw the potential of the XPAG engine and installed it in cars of their own construction, boring it out and incorporating works-provided special equipment. Soon they were producing some seriously powerful and reliable engines. This alarmed the MG Car Company and its parent company, Morris Motors Ltd, who then produced their own Special Tuning Guide for the XPAG engine, describing five different stages of tune to suit everyone from the occasional sporting driver to the racer. More of this in the Tuning chapter.

In 1949 George Phillips ran a special bodied TC at Le Mans, unfortunately being disqualified, but he returned in 1950 and gained second place in the 1500cc class. MG then offered to build a car for him for the 1951 race. This was based on a TD chassis but had a fully-enveloping body (which later inspired the MGA's shape). It suffered mechanical failure in the race and retired.

Phillips, Dick Jacobs (who had raced a TA special) and Ted Lund had works-prepared TCs for

Early days: the team of Cream Cracker trials cars in front of the pits at Donington Park after winning the team prize in the 12 Hour Race in 1937. From left to right are Archie Langley/Johnny "Jesus" Jones, Jack Bastock/Ken Crawford, and Ken MacDermid/ Maurice "The Colonel" Toulmin.

South Africa, 1949. This photograph was taken at the first race meeting at Grand Central Circuit. From left to right are Clive Reeves in a relatively normal looking TC, next to Hilton Gray in a FIAT Special. Next to him is Harry Pierce in an MG special with Y-type front suspension. On the right is Harry Sutcliffe in what looks like a Triple M MG Special.

some 1949 races, and in 1950 got TDs with tuned engines, effectively the first of the TD Mark II models. They came second, third and fourth in the 1500cc class in the *Daily Express* production car race at Silverstone in that year, and later took first, second and third in class in the TT at Dundrod. But competition was stiffening and the next few years saw little works participation in racing. Things changed in 1954, when BMC set up a competitions department. In 1955 a TF 1500 driven by Pat Moss and Pat Faichney came third in the Ladies' Cup in the RAC Rally, three TF 1500s competed in the Circuit of Ireland, Ian and Pat Appleyard coming fourth overall, and in June a class win and the team prize were gained in the Scottish Rally. In the same month MGAs appeared at Le Mans, so the TF had become obsolete.

Immediately after the war and into the mid-1950s TCs and specials with XPAG engines were frequently seen in national racing. Those early days of postwar racing were very free and easy, so that a lot of people were able to enjoy their motor sport, and a number of the drivers went on to star in international motor sport with considerable honour. Peter Arundel raced a black TC in the 1940s and early '50s and went on to race in Formula One with Lotus and others. John Fitch, an American, raced TCs extensively in the United States before being noticed and progressing to faster sports cars. He was a member of the Ford GT40 team at Le Mans and other international sports car races in the mid-1960s.

Phil Hill, another American, also raced Ts before moving into single-seater racing: he joined Ferrari at the end of the 2.5-litre formula and became World Champion.

Another T-type racing exponent in the United States was John Edgar, who was then a distributor for Italmeccanica superchargers, which had magnesium alloy two-lobe rotors. He fitted one of these to his TC. Belt-driven, it ran at speeds up to 12,000rpm, with a 6500rpm limit on the engine and 12psi boost. The compression ratio was reduced to 6:1 and with other modifications the engine gave a peak output of 148bhp – and this as early as 1950.

Edgar was one the first to develop an intercooler for supercharged engines so the induction system was very different. It comprised a single Solex carburetor fitted with a Thompson Products Vitamet meter, which blended water and detergent with the fuel, and an ex-aircraft multi-tube heat exchanger was fitted with an intercooler into the manifold. An electric fuel pump circulated water from a storage tank, packed with dry ice and mounted on the cockpit floor, to the intercooler via a subsidiary radiator mounted on the body side. A similar heat exchanger was fitted to the side of the sump and the air-cooling was sufficient to reduce engine temperature. The water system was pressurized to 7psi and was filled with methylene glycol instead of water, which raised the boiling point to almost 300 degrees Fahrenheit. As a result this engine was extremely reliable while still retaining the standard MG crankshaft, connecting rods and pistons. Edgar also carried out extensive modifications to the suspension and back axle ratio, raising the axle ratio to 4.875:1 and fitting special high-tensile steel half shafts. He installed 12in aircraft-type brakes with light alloy drums and backplates. In the 1950/51 season he scored five first places, three second places, one non-start and one retirement. This would have been against all-comers, often with exotic foreign machinery, so his achievements, and those of Ken Miles as described below, were significant. The 148bhp Edgar obtained was remarkable in those days. The 1500cc-engined XPAGs running in today's racing do achieve about 140bhp, their reliability being derived from steel crankshafts, steel con rods, aircraft style valves with shorter and softer valve springs, and special camshafts.

Ken Miles, from California, who raced TCs before designing his own T-type specials R1 and R2, was also part of the Ford GT sports car team in the 1960s. R1 and R2 used the XPAG engine and other T-type and Y-type components and

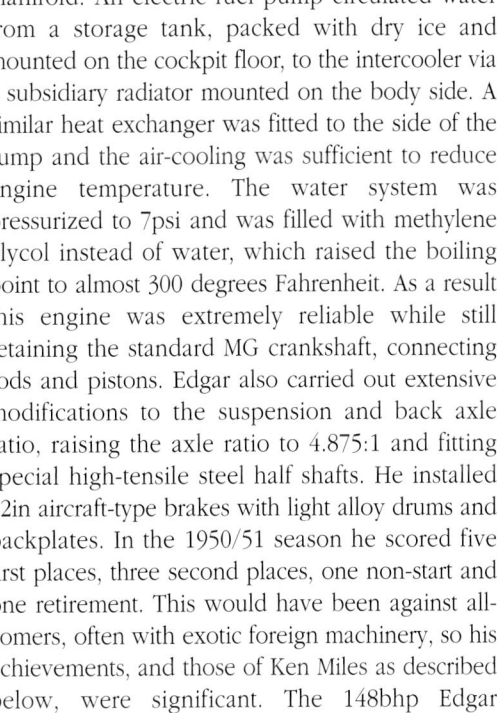

A celebrated MG-powered racer of the early 1950s was this Cooper, registered JOY 500 and extensively campaigned by Cliff Davis. There is more than a little of the contemporary Ferrari in its styling.

MG T SERIES IN DETAIL

Peter Ross at the wheel of Bill Weston's TC at Silverstone during a 6 Hour Relay Race in the 1960s. (Photo Michael Ware)

Shots taken at Relay Races in the 1960s. This one shows my newly supercharged TC next to the immaculate TC of Ken Cheeseman at Oulton Park in 1966.

competed in the under 1500cc class in American sports car racing of the time. R1 had a ladder-framed chassis based on the Emeryson 500cc Formula Three car and front suspension from a Y-type, though only loosely based on this as it had lightweight wheel spindles mated to modified TC front hubs so that it could be adapted to take wire wheels. The Y-type brakes were modified, with twin wheel cylinders and Alfin brake drums, which were available for the TC at that time. Steering was by Morris Minor rack and pinion, with torsion bar front suspension and quarter-elliptic springs at the back adapted from a Morris Oxford. The TC rear axle was fitted with a 4.5:1 ratio. It had mountings welded to it for the shock absorbers and upper radius rods. The chassis was stiff and the suspension was very soft, with all the roll resistance built into the front suspension. Whilst R1 was being built MG had introduced the TD2 engine, which Ken miles incorporated. It was bored out to 1466cc, had a camshaft modified for racing and the compression ratio was 10.5:1. The water passages between the head and the block were blocked off and an external cooling pipe was fitted. With twin 1⅜in SU carburettors the engine developed more than 80bhp at 6000rpm.

R1 had a streamlined body with cycle-type front wings. All the panels were curved in one plane only and there was a complete, flat underpan. The lower part of the body was made from a sheet of aluminum fixed to the edges of the underpan. The spare wheel was mounted vertically on the tail, which was also covered with a single sheet of aluminum, and the radiator was cowled as well.

The car was completed just in time for the 1953 season and in 1954 had a season of uninterrupted wins. Late that year, however, the flywheel bolt sheared, with disastrous results. By then Ken Miles had entered the car in 14 main events, winning 13 and retiring once.

In 1954, with rumours of cycle wings being banned, Ken built his second special, R2. The front suspension was adapted from R1, but to reduce frontal area the driver's seat was mounted lower down. This time there was a spaceframe chassis with an all-enveloping light-gauge aluminum body. The original engine had reached the limit of its development, but Ken's luck was in, for MG had come to Bonneville Salt Flats for an attempt on the Class F endurance record and had brought some spare engines. One of these was apparently "lost" on the return trip, and later reappeared in Ken Miles's workshop!

The rear suspension of R2 incorporated transverse torsion bars with trailing links attached to the rear axle. The links were actually the tie rods from the Morris Minor's front suspension, a modification discovered quite independently by the author when he installed the same tie rods on the back axle of his TC racer! The TC rear axle in R1 had proved somewhat troublesome, so it was replaced by one from a Morris Minor with modified bearing housings enabling TF half shafts, brake backplates and hubs to be used. The TC gearbox was retained as it was extremely robust. The streamlined body dictated that everything be kept as low as possible, and a lot of time went into modifying the inlet

Pete Ross in his TC at Silverstone in 1965...

...and Pete's car later that afternoon, having a new piston fitted!

The paddock at Silverstone in 1966. (Photo Tony Shaw)

manifold so that it was mounted upside down. This involved altering the float chambers so that the carburettors pointed up at the cylinder head instead of looking down at it, and saved some eight inches in height. Unfortunately the exhaust outlets then ran above the carburetors, necessitating a considerable number of heat shields and cooling ducts. The first race was a failure as the engine seized solid. However, R2 went on to be entered in seven main events, five of which it won, taking a second place in the last event.

In Kenya a Colonel Grantham did wonderful things with a cut-about Y-Type chassis, moving the engine and gearbox back 23½ inches! His car was lowered and had a special narrow body with cycle-type front wings. The engine was fitted with 12:1 compression ratio pistons, a big-valve head, 1½in carburettors with 0.125 jets, and ran on 100% methanol. There was one racetrack in Kenya – Langa Langa – and in 1951, first time out, the car won the 1500cc class and lowered the class record by 10 seconds, beating the previous class winners, a Jowett Jupiter and an HRG. Not bad for a home-brewed special!

In Australia wonderful things were being done at this time. The Tomlinson TA had acquired an XPAG and continued to upset the establishment for several years after the war. The original TA engine found its way into another TA, that of Bill McClachlan, which he had converted into a single-seater. The car won club races and was highly placed in major events, finishing second in the NSW Grand Prix in 1947 and ninth in the Australian Grand Prix. After running in the 1948 Australian Grand Prix the engine was taken out and fitted to a Firefly II boat designed by K Barry which broke various World and Australian Water Speed Records. In modern times Roger Waters (not the Pink Floyd one) has fitted a V8 engine to his TC, achieving prodigious speeds racing it, and it

Castle Combe in 1968. Gerry Brown in TC number 14 in one of his first events. He went on to become the man to beat in the 1970s.

Glyn Giusti leads Ron Gammons at Brands Hatch in 1977 or '78.

has been known to win a concours as well.

In Britain, as well as Peter Arundel there were drivers such as Dick Jacobs, who raced a modified TA special as well as TCs before he became a works driver for MG. He was severely injured when he crashed one of the three MGAs in 1955 at Le Mans. He went on to manage other drivers, such as Alan Foster, in his own team of MGs including Z-Type Magnettes, two MGA Twin Cams and subsequently two special-bodied MG Midgets with an aluminum coupé body designed on similar lines to the MGB GT, only smaller and lighter, and these cars, known as the Jacobs Midgets, raced internationally in the early 1960s including the Targa Florio in Sicily. A personal friend of the author, Bill Beedie, raced a TC in national racing in the 1940s and '50s, achieving considerable club success. His car, known as Bluebottle, still exists to this day and was for a time raced in the T-Register Drivers Championship. The author recalls racing against it at Croft in the North East of England during the 1970s.

Towards the end of the 1950s a new generation of T racers started to emerge. These were young men who had acquired T-types and enjoyed using them to their full potential, so a new set of cars and drivers came on the scene. One of these was Derry Dickson with an XPEG-engined TA. Later, men such as Bill Weston, Pete Ross and Roy Brading led the charge with TCs they had developed to their own engine specifications, Roy's car, for instance was supercharged, Pete's car remained unsupercharged and Bill Weston's was also unsupercharged, but they were all playing with different states of cylinder head tune, camshafts, carburetion, etc. The author, who had obtained a

Oulton Park, 1984. John Brigden in Ron Gammons's TC leads Richard Green in his TC on the left and Chris Owen in a supercharged TA. The author is in TA number 5 with Glyn Giusti driving George Edney's TB behind. (Photo Chris Harvey)

TC in 1962 and was exceedingly keen to go motor racing, recalls spectating at Silverstone that year when Bill Weston, in his TC, won a couple of races by a considerable distance, beating MGAs and later T-types with ease. As a result of this the author started competing in 1963 with his TC, and at the same time several other drivers came on the scene with their cars. It was probably in the minds of these drivers that they would use their TCs on the tracks for a year or two before perhaps moving up into say Lotus Sevens and then single-seaters. It was still possible then to use that route to get into national and international racing.

However, at Silverstone in 1963 this group of drivers got together and later on that year formed the MG Car Club T Register. Bill Weston, Ron Gammons (who also had come out in an exceedingly rapid TC as well as driving a TA) and the author were all part of the formation of this register, together with Andrew Roberts. Andrew was sprinting and hillclimbing a TC at the time. He is now an independent motoring journalist, while Ron Gammons has gone on to form his well-known MG restoration and parts business. Both Ron and the author advanced in MG Car Club circles, Ron as Chairman and the writer as Editor of its magazine *Safety Fast!* for 16 years. However, in those days we were all young and idealistic. A Newsletter and Bulletin were produced by the T Register and distributed free of charge to all the T-type owners in the MG Car Club, which was then still run out of its Abingdon office and was well financed. The Bulletin in particular gathered momentum and as a lot of early writers for it were involved in racing T-types quite a lot was written about them. As a result, more drivers started racing, sprinting and hillclimbing their T-types, to the extent that in 1967 a championship was set up for them. This is the MG Car Club T Register Drivers Championship, which resulted in invitations to races organised by other motor clubs and in particular to close relationship with the Bentley Drivers Club which has lasted to the present day.

The grids of T-types were impressive, often numbering between 30 and 40 cars, while the races, especially during the 1960s and 1970s, became the highlight of race meetings and were written and talked about with awe. At one particular meeting at Silverstone when four or five cars had come through the right-hand Woodcote corner flat out, drifting mildly and almost dead heating across the line, Robin Rew in *Autosport*, commented, "If you quail at the sight of a Formula Ford race then you should watch an MG T-type race as an example of what close motor racing really is".

The Championship was divided into classes, so that someone with a fairly ordinary T-type could bring it to the track and although not necessarily going particularly fast could pick up sufficient points to win the Championship. There was also what might be termed a road/race class, in which engines were restricted to 1300cc, unsupercharged, and the cars had to retain all their original wings and trim. Engines could be tuned to Stage 2, with a 9:1 compression ratio. This became a very popular class and frequently produced if not winners, at least runners-up. Class C became the full-race class, allowing the fitment of cycle wings, wider wheels, engines bored out to 1500cc, different camshafts and a whole variety of superchargers. In those early days the cars were still fairly rough and ready but mechanically they were A1, especially after being examined by Fred Matthews, who was a scrutineer at Silverstone and who knew the manufacture of these cars intimately. He put several of us straight before recognising that we were serious, and he became a good friend to many of us. He never neglected his duty however, so presenting one's car to him was always a nerve-wracking business.

As the 1970s rolled into the 1980s the drivers became more affluent as they progressed in their careers, and thus were able to spend more money on their cars, the most obvious manifestation being new paint jobs! There was also a change in the roll-call of drivers: several of the early ones either restricted their activities to one or two events a year or disappeared altogether, while others arrived on the scene having either bought T-types already built up for racing or commissioned their own, so that by the 1990s there was a bigger discrepancy between the faster cars and those that were more traditionally tuned. Modern superchargers

Two years later at the same track. This time it is the author in a newly resprayed TA who has got the jump over Ron Gammons's TF and Richard Green's TC. John Seber in a Wolseley Special is on the outside. Ron's son, Malcolm, follows in his TF. My superb start stood me in good stead for 5 of the 10 laps when Ron finally got by! (Photo Chris Harvey)

appeared, and because there was a decline in the numbers of cars on the grids certain allowances were made to enable cars that did not exactly meet the spirit of the regulations to compete. Nonetheless the T race at Silverstone continues to be the highlight of the MG Car Club's annual festival.

Experience of racing T-types showed that the XPAG engine was exceedingly robust and amenable to considerable development. Initially engines were bored out to 1350cc using Powermax pistons. These were solid-skirt forged pistons with three thin oil rings. They had to be fitted with relatively wide clearances, so engines fitted with them burned a lot of oil and they were not suitable for road use. Subsequently a new series of pistons appeared from the United States which closely replicated the original Aerolite pistons in the early XPAG engines. They were available in sizes from standard up to 0.120in oversize, so 1350cc engines could be bored out to 1370cc. A number of drivers took their engines to this capacity while others developed them further, boring engines out to 1500cc. These were linered, and early ones were prone to failure until it became understood that the liners should be fixed at both top and bottom and sealed properly. In addition it was necessary to support the top deck of the block by inserting a rod through the top of the centre main bearing to support the deck. Steel crankshafts and connecting rods were by then available, together with a wealth of different camshaft profiles.

Just after the war an engineering firm called Laystall Engineering marketed an aluminum cylinder head designed by an engineer called John Lucas. This head was known as the Laystall Lucas cylinder head and it became a prized possession of T-type racers of the 1960s and '70s. However, the heads were made of an aluminum alloy that was not as modern as the times, and most had been skimmed so frequently that they produced compression ratios of 11:1 and upwards! In the 1990s these heads were replicated in a more suitable aluminum alloy, fitted with large valves and bronze valve guides, and appeared on most of the advanced T racers, giving on their own a power boost of 20 per cent or so and contributing to the cooling of the super-tuned engines.

Today T-types continue to race, adding variety to the grids of MG Car Club meetings and other club events. T-types were developed for racing so that they would hold the road and not weave under braking. Although their shape militates against them achieving high speeds, acceleration times have been reduced so that most of these cars can now accelerate from 0-60mph in 7-8 seconds and achieve top speeds in excess of 115 mph.

With an aeroscreen and an open-faced helmet, driving one of these cars with cycle wings gives a tremendous sense of speed and excitement. The suspension will be controlled by anti-tramp arms between the front axle and the chassis, just in front of the driver's door, often a front Panhard rod, and on the rear axle a variety of different linkages, varying from anti-tramp arms to fully-developed Watts linkages. As a result all four wheels stay on the road, braking is stable and progressive and you can steer the car more with the throttle than with the steering wheel.

In the 1960s the drivers dispensed with the standard 19-inch wheels and began to run 15inch or 16inch wheels fitted variously with Dunlop racing tyres, crossply road tyres or even radial tyres. This was the heyday of the Pirelli Cinturato radial, which could be obtained in 16-inch sizes and which the author installed on his car to considerable effect. In the early days brakes were modified by fitting anti-fade brake linings, but as speeds rose the heat generated tended to warp the steel brake drums. After various attempts at skimming the brake drums for a temporary solution, it was eventually discovered that the brake drums fitted to the back axles of the Triumph 2000 saloon were the same size as TA, TB and TC drums and being cast iron retained their shape. Later on, the finned brake drums off Datsun 240Zs were also found to be compatible with T-types and these appeared on several cars, giving them extra cooling for the brakes. One or two people converted their brakes to the two-leading-

The ex-Dick Jacobs YB Coupe, which was raced in the Championship in the late 1970s and early '80s.

A grid of T-types at Silverstone in 1952. Number 17 is a TA driven by Derry Dickson. He later fitted it with an XPEG engine. These days Derry enthusiastically drives a TC. (Photo Guy Griffiths)

shoe arrangement but in general there is no difference in braking effect between the cars, whatever sort of brake drum is fitted.

On supercharged cars cooling was always marginal and frequently radiators would be re-cored with an extra row in them. Today, money has raised the stakes and aluminum radiator cores are now available.

There was considerable alarm some 25 years ago when it was thought that metal fatigue might be entering the frame, and a lot of research was carried out into the tempering of TC stub axles. They do have a tendency to break, but usually at a low speed and on a road car that has endured a lot of pothole activity over many years, with the result that the nearside stub axle would sometimes collapse at an inopportune moment when negotiating into a parking spot. However, the research indicated that the stub axles were normally robust, and with regular crack testing there has never been a problem in T racing.

The chassis can also break, either in the middle where the boxing finishes or at the top of the dumb irons, again where the boxing finishes. To avert this an extra sheet of metal can be welded in to make a fish-tailed end to the boxing. A break at the front can have comic, if disastrous, consequences on a TA or TB, as the springs can slide out of their trunnions, leaving the whole front suspension and front of the chassis to wander free.

During the 40 years there have been several crashes in T-type racing, usually brought about by over-exuberance, but none of the drivers involved has received any serious injury despite several lurid rolls and high-speed impacts. In the early days, when we had no seatbelts or rollover bars, drivers were lucky not to be seriously injured in such incidents, and subsequently, as rollover bars became standard together with full-harness seat belts, injuries from accidents were minimized. The author was involved in two serious accidents in 1975 and 1993. On the first occasion he lost control of his TC at Cadwell Park. This accident was subsequently attributed to the breakage of a steering balljoint. The car hit a bank and overturned, shedding wheels and bending the TC chassis into a Z shape, yet the only injuries sustained were bruises from the seatbelts. In the second accident, at Silverstone, a spinning car was rammed by the author's car, which then took off over the back of it after a high-speed impact. Again, despite the very violent deceleration, the author escaped with seatbelt bruises and a severely bruised right foot from the impact with the brake pedal. It proved therefore that these cars are deceptively strong and that motor racing, even if it is dangerous, is survivable! Through his involvement with T racing, the author made many friends and derived an enjoyment which has not been matched by anything else.

Chapter Eight

Evolution of a Racer

This section contains a photographic record of the development of a T-type which the author raced and which now continues to be raced in the hands of Frank Albers, an American who has been living in Yorkshire for the last 20 or so years. What follows is the author's impressions of a lap of the International Circuit at Silverstone – any race there, not any particular occasion, say in 2000. Imagine the track being bathed in sunshine with a light north-easterly wind.

The day starts early, towing the car to arrive at Silverstone in the paddock in time for scrutineering. After a round of hellos to friends and after slotting the trailer into a confined space in the paddock, the car is unloaded and then started. The starting procedure for this particular car is effected from outside. The 1¾in carburettor sticks out of the bonnet side and has the usual T-type choke mechanism but with no cable. To start the engine I stand half way between the carburettor and the dashboard so that I can reach the starting button with my left hand and with the right hand operate the choke. The engine fires immediately, and after a few seconds settles into a slightly lumpy idle at round 2000rpm. After emptying the car of any unnecessary detritus such as spare wheels for the trailer, I venture forth in it out of the paddock and join the queue for scrutineering. This is very much a stop-go procedure but eventually I reach the scrutineering bay, handing in my signing-on sheet to the scrutineer, who then proceeds to inspect the car, ensuring that all the fuel lines are in place, that there are no leaks, that the wheels, tyres and suspension are all tight and legal. He tests the seatbelts, possibly the brakes and the lights, and also checks that the overalls and helmet you are wearing are compliant with the latest regulations. These days it is highly unusual for the scrutineer to fail a racing T-type as they have been honed to perfection over many years, so at the completion of the scrutineering I am handed a scrutineering label which I affix to the inside of the car in a prominent position so it can be seen later by the start line marshals.

With this hurdle crossed, the car is driven back to its spot in the paddock and checked for sufficient fuel, water and oil, to await practice. Nerves are on edge, despite nearly 40 years' experience, as I put on the racing overalls and driving boots and make sure that my gloves and crash helmet are safely in the car. When the time comes, I and all the others drive off in a riot of noise to the assembly area for the first practice session.

Further time elapses while the previous practice session is run and closed and our scrutineering labels are checked. We are warned that we will be sent out shortly, so we don our crash helmets and gloves and sit in our cars strapped in full harness seatbelts. Then it is our turn to be summoned on to the track. This is a liberating moment! There is always a sense of fun as we go out on to the track hitting the throttle and making our way round the Luffield curves before accelerating out of Luffield Two into Woodcote Corner, which on this first lap is not necessarily taken flat out, but then it's maximum revs down the pit straight before jostling for the left hand side of the track, dabbing the brakes and turning the car into Copse Corner. Copse is an immensely fast, enjoyable right-hand corner where it's very easy to drift the car out just so much so that it hits the rumble strips. Any further and I am in the gravel and at the end of my drive!

The next corners are the left-handed Maggots, followed by the Becketts right, left and right and the final left hander, so I attempt to sidle my way into the right-hand side of the track in order to get a good line through Maggots, which can be taken flat out, and if I am very brave I don't brake going into the Becketts complex. There are other cars around so I need to dab the brakes in order to get into position before sweeping through the left and then tight right-hander, which calls for third gear, before accelerating hard leftwards and out on the main straight. Now it's back into top gear and letting the revs get to my rev limit of 6400rpm, or 112mph on this particular gearing. Much sooner than I anticipate I am into the right-hand corner of the Abbey complex. The brakes have to work extremely hard here, and due to a quirk in the road surface it seems I am never going to stop. But I do, or at least I slow sufficiently to engage third gear round the right-hander, clipping the left verge through the left-hand section of Abbey and accelerating again up to full speed towards the sweeping right curve at Bridge, where I dive under the Bridge, sweep right and come up over a brow somewhat abruptly into the Brook-lands and Luffield complex. A lot of speed is carried through the first left-hander, the car drifting out to the right in order to take a tight line through the left-hand Brooklands before jinking out to the left again into Luffield One and Luffield Two, where the car will drift out to the left, running up over the rumble strips. Then hard acceleration, so that this time the car is really flying as I go through Woodcote Corner at around 6000rpm. In the wet it is important to be rather delicate at this particular corner as it is so fast, and with adhesion reduced the car will easily slide. I now arrive at Copse at full speed and the lap starts all over again.

By the time eight or nine laps of practice have been completed, the car is hot and so am I. The weather is very warm so the brakes are beginning to fade, and I'm relieved to see the chequered flag. I pull back into the paddock for the car to cool down and be got ready for the afternoon's race.

For the race the procedure is similar except that you then have grid positions based on your morning practice times. When you are called out you take up your allocated position on the starting grid. A minute or so later you are released under the Green Flag for the warm-up lap, this procedure being no different from what you see on the television before a Formula 1 race, and the start is similar too, so that when all the cars are back on the grid the lights go from red to green and the race is on. The circuit is exactly the same as it was in the morning although it may have some extra rubber down on the corners. In race conditions, of course, cars are all around you. The priority is to overtake them and not let them overtake you. For 10 laps it's a game of cat and mouse between closely-matched cars, often racing in very close company so that lines might have to be adapted through any corner on any lap. Assuming that nothing has broken or fallen off, 10 laps of racing soon pass, and once back in the paddock the cars are all parked up, with the drivers congregating to congratulate each other or bemoan circumstances, depending on the result. All those who didn't win have, needless to say, plenty of excuses to offer.

For me racing was a wonderful hobby. May it long continue!

In 1969 I bought an extractor exhaust manifold from Derrington's, then a well-known MG accessory supplier. This meant I had to have a new inlet manifold between the blower and the head. Roy Brading had built one for his similar car, but I was in Cambridge and he was in Somerset. I asked Brian Lister of Lister Engineering to design me something and he produced a one-off manifold for me. It was basically a balanced collecting box. You can see it here. You can also see twin fuel lines, the oil feed to the supercharger's nosepiece and the 1¾in SU carburettor. At this time I still used a single vee-belt to drive the supercharger.

This is the TC I first acquired in October 1962. At that time it was very much a standard road car. In July 1963 I entered it for a hill climb at Firle on the South Downs near Lewes. Here it is approaching the top bend to record the slowest T-type time of the day! (Photo James Brymer)

The TC at Silverstone in May 1964 at the MG Car Club's annual race meeting. It was running on borrowed 16in wheels with a Stage 1A cylinder head, 8:1 compression ratio and large valves. It failed miserably as the spark plugs I had fitted caused a serious misfire. I finished next to last by dint of a daring overtaking manoeuvre at the last corner.

EVOLUTION OF A RACER

By September 1964 I had sorted the car out. fitted some rather crude cycle wings to the front and was in search of more power.

In 1965 I fitted a Marshall J75 supercharger kit designed for the TC. I installed it in the car behind our house in the centre of Cambridge and the first time I drove it I was overwhelmed by its increased power. I went back to Firle that year and won the class, in the wet.

151

This shot of me was taken at Stapleford hill climb in Essex. It was very wet and the water off the front wheels was stinging my face. I was the only T-type driver in the class and beat a Lotus Elan and a TVR. I felt quite good, as this performance confirmed my ability in the wet.

By 1966 I had got out the Valspar again, this time Red. Here we are at Prescott hill climb in Gloucestershire.

Silverstone, and it's Copse corner...

...and Woodcote, about to be eaten up by the single-seater ex-Monaco Engineering K3 in the hands of Syd Beer.

A bit later, in 1968, a driver named Dave Clewley arrived on the scene. He was naturally quick and made T racing look easy with his relaxed style. At this time he was learning, and in this shot I had driven round outside him at Woodcote to beat him to the line.

This was also taken around those times. Again I am enjoying myself in the wet!

EVOLUTION OF A RACER

In 1971 I added a roll over bar and started towing the car to race meetings, then in 1972 came my finest hour when I won the T-Register's Drivers Championship outright. I received sponsorship from Duckhams which consisted of four one-gallon tins of 20/50 oil, brake fluid and grease for the season. This photo was taken then, with an oil cooler added.

Here is the car at Prescott in 1970 after a proper respray in Blue Royale at Syd Beer's garage.

155

My first accident in the TC was in October 1964. I went into a ditch when fog coated both sides of the windscreen and my glasses simultaneously. The hole in the front sidescreen was made by my head!

The second crash in 1975 was nasty. It was at Cadwell Park in Lincolnshire. I was near the front when the TC took off on a journey of its own and headed off across the grass. It would not respond to the steering, slammed into the bank and somersaulted over backwards. I came to hanging upside down from my safety belt. My car was a write off. The chassis was Z-shaped and one wheel complete with king pin was detached. You can't see much in this photo, but close study shows a twisted chassis. The accident was caused by a broken steering balljoint, probably caused in a small accident at a hillclimb a month or two earlier.

I was undeterred. A year or two earlier I had bought a TA chassis. That winter I transplanted the TC body on to it, rewired it and put the engine, gearbox and back axle on it. The car emerged in 1976 as TA 0448, DGH 567, instead of TC 1730, JKJ 748. My TC having been known as "The Old Nail", the TA became the "New Nail".

By 1979 another respray was needed. This time it was done by one of my clients. Two-tone schemes were popular amongst us then, so mine was done in Grey and Blue. I was still receiving help from Duckhams, as this photo at Brands Hatch in around 1980 shows. By this time I was experimenting with toothed belt drive to the supercharger, and low-compression VA pistons combined with an 11:1 compression ratio Laystall head, an original 1940s one. The car was sporadically very fast, up amongst the leaders, or blowing up.

In 1985 I resprayed the car myself in a shade of blue, added some "go-faster" stripes, and rebuilt the engine as a 1350 with Powermax pistons. The toothed belt remained until it had broken everything it could in the drive train, finally reaching the supercharger gears, when it wore a Woodruff key and the rotors touched. After that the supercharger produced reduced boost. I then fitted a multi-vee belt and pulleys, and geared the supercharger up to run a bit faster.

Now began a Purple Patch in my racing career, as I started regularly to qualify on the front row and finish on the podium, with at least a couple of wins in the late 1980s. The car remained competitive until October 1993, when disaster struck again. Before describing that, a look at the car in these halcyon days: here I am duelling with my great friend, the late Malcolm Hogg, in his TF 1500 at Silverstone in 1987.

In 1996 I was delighted to be invited to race at the Coys International Historic Festival at Silverstone. We had to fit swept front wings for this meeting, as you can see here.

In 1993 I had my last racing accident. It was in practice at the Eights Club end-of-season race meeting. I had entered a handicap race for similarly powered cars, but the authorities saw fit to allow a TIGA rear-engined sports-racer to practise out of session with us. Unfortunately it was in the hands of a relative novice. He spun it in the Luffield complex in front of me, got going again, passed me down the Pit Straight and disappeared round Copse before I got there. He had spun it again and was tucked up in the inside of the corner, well out of the racing line, when he suddenly reversed, right in front of me. There was nothing I could do, though I thought at the time I could steer round the car. Subsequent viewing of the video of the accident showed how impossible that thought was. I could do no more than jam on my brakes, and I hit the TIGA broadside on, just behind the driver, more by luck than judgement. Immediately I heard a shout of "Fire" which made me get out in a hurry. This time the marshals were quickly on the scene and the doctor was there, first attending to the TIGA's driver, still in his car, and then to me. I was certified OK, which was more than could be said for my poor car. The other driver was OK too, I was relieved to find out later. It could have been so much worse. The TA

Two views of the engine compartment. The first shows the engine around 1995, illustrating the cut-away bulkhead, twin fuel pumps and ex-Wolseley 4/44 1370cc engine. The second is from 1999. Note the multi-vee belt drive to the supercharger and the revised and neater twin fuel lines.

EVOLUTION OF A RACER

Not a pretty sight! The chassis was twisted but saveable and the radiator, shell and headlamps were crushed and some timbers were loosened in the body. The second shot shows the chassis, stripped for repair at Len Bull's workshop in Essex.

was in a poor way. Its chassis was split open at the front, twisted but essentially straight, the radiator, shell and headlamps were all crushed, and some timbers were loose in the body. As you can see, the car needed a great deal of restoration. So did I, as I subsequently suffered from a very deep bruise to the ball of my right foot, caused by the jar on the brake pedal when I hit the other car. It took most of that winter to cure itself. The photo shows what the damage looked like from the outside.

After that I never achieved the places I had before, and due to a variety of reasons my appearances gradually tailed off. I still enjoyed some good racing but gradually slipped down the field as the bureaucracy of racing increased and circuits lost their souls. Silverstone in 1963 was an open, friendly place. By the 1990s it had assumed the appearance of a prison camp. I was glad to retire in 2002. It was a world away from the golden age of the 1960s, '70s and '80s. T racing had altered too. Open trailers were few and far between, let alone tow cars, with Winnebago-type vehicles the norm. The sport had changed from a young man's day out to a serious affair involving heavy financial outlay. I sold the car in 2003, and it continues to be raced by Frank Albers. It was some car.

April 1994, in conditions I really enjoyed, at Snetterton. (Photo Eric Metcalfe)

159

MG T SERIES IN DETAIL

Back at home in early 1994 after its rebuild, with final tracking to do.

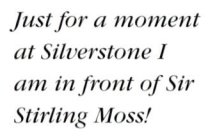

Just for a moment at Silverstone I am in front of Sir Stirling Moss!

Out at Mallory Park in 1995.

In the paddock at Silverstone in 1990.

160

At Silverstone again in early 1993. (Photo Mary Harvey)

Chapter Nine

Tuning T-types

In 1949 MG published a Special Tuning booklet for the XPAG engine as fitted to the TB and TC. As mentioned earlier, the long-stroke TA engine was never very susceptible to tuning apart from maintaining the optimum carburettor and ignition settings. The booklet described what was necessary to tune the XPAG engine for Stages 1 to 5, and the instructions are summarised below.

Stage 1 involved raising the compression ratio to 8.6:1 by removing 3/32in from the cylinder head face, giving a finished depth to the head of 74.37mm. Exhaust and inlet ports should be ground out and matched to the manifold ports. Washers should be fitted under the cylinder head nuts, and packing pieces under the rocker shaft pillars to retain valve geometry. The standard head gasket and carburettors are retained, the latter with 0.090in jets and ES needles, tappets are set to 0.022in and ignition to TDC.

For Stage 2 the compression ratio was raised further, to 9.3:1, achieved by machining ⅛in off the standard cylinder head to give a finished head depth of 73.575mm. 36mm inlet and 34mm exhaust valves were fitted, which necessitated cutting back parts of the combustion chamber wall, and stronger valve springs (150lb open tension) were specified. Again, the standard head gasket and carburettors were retained, with the same needle/jet combination as in Stage 1, and the same tappet and ignition settings. It was noted that removing the cooling fan would liberate an extra 1bhp, and that while the tappets could be set to 0.019in for quietness, that would be at a cost of approximately 1bhp. Larger 1½in carburettors could optionally be fitted.

Stage 3 demanded quite challenging modifications including raising the compression ratio to an astronomical 12:1 (with the standard head) by the use of special pistons, available from the factory, and running on a fuel brew that included 80% methanol. An extra SU petrol pump was recommended, with GK needles for the standard carburettors, 0.100jets, and SU T3 needle and seat assemblies for the float chambers. Timing was to be set to 4 degrees ATDC. The larger 1½ SUs were again optional, and larger valves could be fitted too.

A Shorrock supercharger kit was the basis of Stage 4. It was an eccentric vane type mounted on the inlet manifold, driven by twin belts from the crankshaft pulley, and designed to give a large increase in power at lower and medium engine speeds. A 1½in SU carburettor was recommended, with an RLS needle and 0.090in jet.

Stage 5 combined Stage 4's supercharger with the 9.3:1 compression ratio and larger valves of Stage 2. A larger 0.125in jet and VG needle were specified for the carburettor, along with an additional fuel pump. For yet more power, a 1¾in SU was recommended.

The question of power outputs from the Stage 1 to Stage 5 modifications is confused by MG's fuel recommendations. Petrol in the UK at that time being of very low octane rating, various blends were suggested for the various stages, involving petrol, benzol and methanol. Using these fuels MG estimated the maximum outputs of the modified engines as:

Stage 1	60bhp @ 6000rpm
Stage 2	61-68bhp @ 6000rpm depending on carburettor size and fuel mix
Stage 3	74bhp @ 5800rpm with standard valves
	76bhp @ 5800rpm with the larger valves
Stage 4	70bhp @ 5000-6000rpm
Stage 5	88bhp @ 5500-6000rpm
	97.5bhp @ 6000rpm with 1¾in carburettor

Another tuning booklet was issued in 1954, giving details of Stage 1 to 3 tuning for the XPAG engine in the TF 1250 and Stage 1 to 4 for the XPEG engine of the TF1500.

1250

Stage 1 for the 1250 involved the same machining of the head face as for the earlier cars to give an 8.6:1 compression ratio. The same cleaning up and polishing of ports manifold and head are recommended. The standard – now 1¼in – SUs are retained, fitted with GJ needles and 0.90in jets. Tappets are set at 0.012in and ignition at TDC.

Stage 2 on the 1250 engine includes an increase in compression ratio to 9.3:1, again with the same machining as on the earlier engines. Settings and carburetion were as for Stage 1.

A special camshaft for the 1250, numbered AEG122, available from the factory, was specified for Stage 3, along with the 9.3:1 compression ratio. Tappets were set to 0.019in, timing was set to TDC, the oil pressure was increased, and a special distributor (Lucas 40441A) was suggested. GJ was the carburettor needle specified.

1500

Stage 1 involved machining 0.020in off the head face – finished head thickness 76.25mm – to give an 8.6:1 compression ratio, plus the usual polishing and matching. GJ needles and 0.090jets were specified for the standard carburettors, with tappets set at 0.012in and timing at TDC.

For Stage 2, 0.050in is removed from the standard head face, to raise the compression ratio to 9.3:1. The finished head thickness is 75.5mm and other recommendations are the same as for Stage 1.

Stage 3 sees the compression ratio raised to 9.45:1 by removing 0.068in from the standard head, leaving a finished head thickness of 75.16mm. The same special camshaft as for the Stage 3 1250 is fitted, and other specified modifications are also the same, except that LSI carburettor needles are listed.

For Stage 4 the owner is required to make up (or have someone make up) a four-pipe extractor exhaust manifold. A drawing is provided. This manifold is to be added to the modifications for Stage 3.

In the final section of the 1954 Tuning Booklet there is extensive advice on racing tune for the 1500 engine, involving a 10.7:1 compression ratio, shortening the pushrods, a high-overlap camshaft (168551) from the factory, 1¾in carburettors, the four-pipe extractor exhaust and, for streamlined bodywork, an airbox for the carburettors. The Booklet warns that the amount of metal to be removed from the cylinder head for the increase in compression ratio, 0.068in, is the absolute maximum, and that "some erratic running may occur below 2000rpm".

By 1954, when this Tuning Booklet was published, 90 octane fuel was available, and there is no discussion of home-brewed fuel mixes. Outputs based on the use of 90 octane petrol were given as:

1250 Stage 1	61bhp @ 5000rpm
1250 Stage 2	64bhp @ 5500-6000rpm
1250 Stage 3	66bhp @ 5800-6300rpm
1500 Stage 1	65bhp @ 5000-5000rpm
1500 Stage 2	67bhp @ 5500-6000rpm
1500 Stage 3	70bhp @ 5800-6300rpm
1500 Stage 4	72-73bhp @ 5800-6300rpm
1500 Racing Tune	79bhp @ 6000rpm with 1½in carburettors
	82bhp @ 6300rpm with 1¾in carburettors

Tuning today

Most of what follows is derived from racing experience. The first thing to bear in mind is that increased capacity increases power and torque. The standard 1250cc engine is respec-table as far as it goes, but an increase in bore size by 0.100in is the first sensible move anyone can make. The engine is bored to 69.4mm to produce 1348cc, and in theory all the XPAG blocks should bore out to this capacity. However the best block to use, if increasing the capacity to this extent, is the late TD2 block carried forward into the 1250cc TF range and also used in the Wolseley 4/44. It is not necessary to line these blocks unless there has been a previous failure. To be on the safe side, on oval water hole XPAG blocks it might be advisable to line the bores.

If adapting a Wolseley 4/44 block, it is necessary to fit the appropriate front engine mounting plate, block the dipstick hole on the offside front and drill the blanked-off boss on the nearside. The other thing you need is a TC/TD/TF Sump. Before indulging in any of this, establish what the current cylinder capacity of your engine is.

The next stage to consider is engine breathing. It is important to polish the inlet ports on the XPAG head by turning the boss in the centre of the port, through which the cylinder head stud runs, into a point. Larger valves should be fitted, with heads 2mm wider than standard, and they should be made of current high-specification steel In place of the standard valve springs it is now possible to install modern springs which are considerably shorter than the standard ones and are fitted using aluminium spacers.

You should fit 1½in SU carburettors; another major benefit would be an extractor exhaust manifold as the standard one is very restrictive.

The compression ratio may be raised to at least 9:1 but again you must establish what compression ratio your particular cylinder head is, so I will not define how many thousands of an inch should be milled off the head. If you have a completely standard head, to raise the compression ratio to 9:3:1 you mill ⅛in off it. The depth between the top and bottom faces is then 73.575 mm. On a standard head this is 76.7mm. Armed with this information you can calculate how much has been milled off your head. The volumetric capacity of the combustion chamber can be established using a pipette. Then you open up the chambers where possible to equalise the capacity of each chamber. It is possible to buy a new replica Laystall-Lucas aluminium cylinder head which incorporates all the above.

The type of camshaft to choose depends on what you intend to use the car for. For general road use there is nothing to better the original TD2/TF/Wolseley 4/44 camshaft, which has a 5/45/45/5 timing and a 0.012in tappet clearance. Various other camshaft profiles, including the American-made Crane camshafts, are available from specialists. You need to discuss the exact camshaft specification you need with your engine modifier, as obviously racing and sprinting demand different breathing qualities from general fast road use. Use the later type rocker shafts and rocker gear as the rockers have slightly longer bosses and are not prone to so much wear as the earlier type. A point to watch is the cam followers, which should not be pitted or worn. The face against which the cam turns should be of a uniform polish, indicating that it is turning as well as lifting. The followers can be lightened slightly and it is sensible to mill a channel vertically down the cam follower to allow extra lubrication, as the only lubrication to the camshaft is provided by oil dripping down from the cylinder head.

It is important to ensure that the engine remains cool running. A useful aid to this is to have your radiator re-cored with an extra row so it becomes a three-row radiator.

The standard distributors will work well with an engine such as I have described for road use, but again there are special distributors available for competition use. Spark plug choice is important: the author favours NGK plugs. If you have a half-inch reach head then the BP6HS is the sparking plug to consider, and if you use the long-reach head the BP6ES. As with an ordinary road engine, ensure that the coil is working well and the points are set correctly.

It makes sense to fit a second fuel pump, which in the case of TCs, TDs and TFs will necessitate an extra petrol line which you can plumb into the bottom of the tank in place of the drain plug.

An engine to the above specification would probably produce maybe not far short of 100bhp, certainly 80bhp. At this level you can safely use your existing crankshaft and connecting rods.

Race Tuning up to 140bhp

If you are developing an engine purely for racing you can either adopt the 1350cc route and fit a supercharger, or take the engine out to 1500cc normally aspirated. As previously stated, taking an XPAG out to 1500cc is fraught with difficulty and correspondingly very expensive.

A 1500cc engine like this should be fitted with 1¼in carburettors. An aluminium lightweight multi-core radiator, and an oil cooler, would make sense. It is possible to fit an oil cooler to any of the XPAG cars, as sandwich plate adaptors are readily available and the hoses – as well as the cooler itself – can be sourced from an MGB parts supplier. If possible, the engine should have a finned aluminium sump to provide extra cooling, and if you can find one of the later TF 10-pint sumps then fit that.

A supercharger fitted to a 1350cc engine or even a well-developed and tuned 1500cc engine will add at least 30 per cent to any given bhp rating in the XPAG range. A supercharged engine needs a 1¾in SU carburettor with a 0.100in jet and a needle between RA and RC. A supercharged 1350 unit can show as much as 140bhp, depending on the make and model of supercharger fitted.

There was a time in T racing when anything went as far as superchargers were concerned. Larger and larger Shorrocks vane type units were used, positioned behind the engine on the bulkhead and driven by a long shaft off the front of the crankshaft. Carburettors as big as 2in were fitted. Various large Wade rotor-type superchargers also appeared, together with modern equivalents such as the Volumex, Eaton and Sprintex. The last named were especially contentious when they came to be fitted to the already very fast cars of David Clewley and Paul Smeeth. The racing of that time assumed a Schumacher-type complexion, making T racing for the first time very predictable and eventually somewhat boring. The Sprintex supercharger has now been banned from T racing.

The Eaton supercharger, however, has a much more traditional build and is increasingly becoming the preferred equipment. It can be sourced new as it is supplied to manufacturers such as Jaguar and Aston Martin. Neither is it particularly expensive, but it does need its own oil system, together with manifolds for both the carburettor and connection to the engine.

If you have the XPAG engine fully tuned, with a steel crankshaft and steel connecting rods, lightened valve gear and strengthened valve materials, etc., it is capable of revving to in excess of 7000rpm. It is sensible to limit the revs of an engine with a standard crankshaft to 6400rpm, but even this on a 4.67:1 final drive ratio will give a TA, TB or TC a top speed of 112–115mph. If you are retaining the existing crankshaft and con rods it is important to have them Tuftrided for extra strength. Whatever you are using, it is important to have the whole of the bottom end balanced, from the clutch forward to the front pulley, together with the con rods and pistons. It is amazing how smooth the XPAG engine becomes when it has been fully balanced. An unbalanced standard crankshaft will break if revved above 5800rpm more than once or twice!

Whilst this chapter is basically devoted to engine tuning it is important to note that without a sound chassis, properly sprung, and brakes and steering in top-notch condition, just tuning the engine is a recipe for disaster. On the TA, TB and TC it is sensible to replace the cast steel brake drums with cast iron drums or Alfin or Datsun finned drums. It is important to fit anti-fade linings both front and rear, but there is no need to alter the position of the brake master cylinder. Use racing brake fluid to at least DOT4 rating, make sure that it is changed every year and also check that the wheel cylinders front and rear are dry and unseized. A competition car laid up between say November and February can easily lose its brakes over the winter.

Another wise modification to the braking system is to discard the rubber hoses and fit braided steel hoses instead. These can also be used for oil and petrol pipes, though this is not recommended for competition use as black rubber pipes aid cooling. The wheel sizes most commonly used are 15 x 5½J or 15 x 6J, and the preferred tyre at the moment is Avon All Weather in a 175 x 70 size.

The TC gearbox is suitable for transmitting up to 150bhp and is obviously retained in the TB and TC models. It can replace the TA gearbox if fitted in conjunction with the XPAG engine, and is also used in place of the standard gearbox on the TD and TF, which has weak first and reverse gears.

The standard TA/TB/TC rear axle ratio of 5.125:1 is too low. In its place one can install the 4.89:1 TA unit, and it is also now possible to acquire a higher ratio of 4.67:1. This enables second gear in particular to be held for considerably longer and is therefore of great effect in hairpin and other low-speed corners. In addition it gives 5 per cent higher speeds in third and fourth gears, so at 6500rpm top speed in a TC could be 119mph.

Alternatively, it is not difficult to replace the final drive with a Ford unit. You retain the existing axle casing and fit a final drive unit from the rear wheel drive Ford Escort, for which ratios ranging from 4.4:1 up to 5.1:1 can be obtained. The Ford crownwheel and pinion are considerably stronger than the MG spiral bevel unit. The Ford differential will fit into the MG axle casing with some adjustment of the spacing of the ring of retaining bolts. On the TD and TF it is possible to remove the whole rear axle and replace it with an MGA unit, for which ratios down to 4.3:1 are available, together with an easily removable diff.

For competition purposes the standard lever arm dampers are replaced by Spax adjustable telescopic units, which are fitted to triangulated brackets attached to the existing original shock absorber brackets on the chassis. The tops of the telescopic shock absorbers are just underneath the hatch over the back axle, but the units are tall and span the rear of the axle, so if the brake pipes are not moved they will soon be broken by the up-and-down movement of the axle relative to the shock absorbers. This applies to the TA, TB and TC, and the solution is to re-route the brake pipes across the front of the rear axle, with the flexible hoses joined to them at the front of the axle too.

If preparing a TA/TC for racing it is important to reduce the amount of body roll and to improve traction. At the front the first thing to do is to fit rose-jointed anti-tramp arms from the front axle, just inboard of the kingpins, to the chassis, approximately where the front bulkhead mounting brackets are fitted. These arms locate the axle fore and aft and prevent it from winding up under braking, with all the attendant instability. A Panhard rod can also be usefully fitted, running from a bracket attached to the base of the offside front chassis over the front axle to a bracket attached to the spring hanger on the nearside. This helps to restrict sideways movement of the axle.

At the back there are various schools of thought. The writer favoured a pair of anti-tramp arms attached to the back spring hanger and running to the chassis just as near as possible to the front spring mount. The arms were sourced from the front suspension of a Morris Minor! They prevented wheel spin and produced a great deal of extra traction. Others favour Watts linkages across the axle and/or a Panhard rod. The rear suspension can be usefully softened by removal of one of the spring leaves, with final adjustment using the shock absorber adjusters. Conversely at the front, certainly on the TC, it is helpful to place an extra leaf in the front springs. The TA and TB have extra leaves to start with.

All these modifications, together with 15in wheels, enhance the already excellent road-holding qualities of these cars and, as most racetrack surfaces are very smooth, enable T-Types to outcorner much newer (and in their owners' eyes superior) cars. This might explain why MG T-Types consistently finish much higher up the order of a mixed-marque race than you might expect from just reading the programme.

Appendices

Production Numbers

TA

The prototype T-Types were built in 1936. TA251, registered CJO 618, was built on 3 March and TA252 (CJO 617) was built on 3 April. Production commenced on 25 June.

1936
25 June	TA0253
26 June	TA0272
2 July	TA0273
29 July	TA0386
18 August	TA0387
26 August	TA0490
1 September	TA0491
30 September	TA0685
5 October	TA0686
28 October	TA0820
3 November	TA0821
30 November	TA0955
8 December	TA0956
23 December	TA1015

1937
6 January	TA1016
18 January	TA1063
8 February	TA1064
23 February	TA1095
1 March	TA1096
31 March	TA1205
2 April	TA1206
29 April	TA1259
4 May	TA1260
19 May	TA1411
1 June	TA1412
29 June	TA1547
6 July	TA1548
27 July	TA1628
August	TA1629-TA1723
9 September	TA1724
29 September	TA1765
6 October	TA1766
27 October	TA1865
3 November	TA1866
30 November	TA1980
7 December	TA1981
20 December	TA2043

1938
19 January	TA2044
26 January	TA2083
2 February	TA2084
23 February	TA2143
1 March	TA2144
29 March	TA2284
4 April	TA2285
26 April	TA2374
2 May	TA2375
23 May	TA2459
1 June	TA2460
28 June	TA2509
5 July	TA2510
26 July	TA2549
15 August	TA2550
31 August	TA2612
5 September	TA2613
27 September	TA2712
3 October	TA2713
31 October	TA2857
1 November	TA2858
29 November	TA2962
6 December	TA2963

1939
30 January	TA3073
6 February	TA3074
27 February	TA3143
6 March	TA3144
28 March	TA3238
3 April	TA3239
17 April	TA3253

It is interesting to note that in December and January 1938/39 only two cars were produced. The MG Car Company always had a reputation for good worker relations, so it is doubted that this will have been this caused by a strike; it may just have been down to an extended Christmas holiday or possibly a lack of orders from dealers.

Exactly 3000 TAs were produced.

TB

1939
11 May	TB0253
25 May	TB0360
7 June	TB0361
28 June	TB0425
4 July	TB0426
25 July	TB0505
23 August	TB0506
30 September	TB0532
1 October	TB0533

Production finished a few days later with TB0610. By then the war was in full swing.
Total TB production was 379 cars.

TC

Although, as you will have read, the TC was announced in October 1945, the first ones were actually built in September, although the production date of TC0251 is not known exactly. However, on 17 September production started with TC0252 and by the 28 September they had reached TC0272.

1945
16 October	TC0273
30 October	TC0285
1 November	TC0286
26 November	TC0315
6 December	TC0316
21 December	TC0351

1946		**1948**		**TD**	
1 January	TC0352	5 January	TC4412		
31 January	TC0432	29 January	TC4667	**1949**	
5 February	TC0433	2 February	TC4668	10 November	TD/0251
28 February	TC0512	26 February	TC4902	25 November	TD/0273
5 March	TC0513	1 March	TC4903	5 December	TD/0274
27 March	TC0600	31 March	TC5140	20 December	TD/0348
1 April	TC0601	1 April	TC5141		
30 April	TC0711	30 April	TC5397	**1950**	
1 May	TC0712	4 May	TC5398	2 January	TD/0349
31 May	TC0871	28 May	TC5608	31 January	TD/0612
3 June	TC0872	1 June	TC5609	1 February	TD/0613
28 June	TC1031	30 June	TC5911	28 February	TD/0838
7 July	TC1032	1 July	TC5912	1 March	TD/0839
25 July	TC1181	23 July	TC6150	31 March	TD/1173
12 August	TC1182	10 August	TC6151	3 April	TD/1174
29 August	TC1301	31 August	TC6374	28 April	TD/1469
3 September	TC1302	1 September	TC6375	1 May	TD/1470
28 September	TC1501	30 September	TC6701	31 May	TD/1846
2 October	TC1502	1 October	TC6702	1 June	TD/1847
31 October	TC1711	29 October	TC6976	30 June	TD/2320
1 November	TC1712	3 November	TC6977	3 July	TD/2321
29 November	TC1887	26 November	TC7244	28 July	TD/2722
2 December	TC1888	1 December	TC7245	14 August	TD/2723
31 December	TC2051	24 December	TC7502	31 August	TD/3058
				1 September	TD/3059
1947		**1949**		29 September	TD/3592
1 January	TC2052	5 January	TC7503	2 October	TD/3593
31 January	TC2281	31 January	TC7775	31 October	TD/4123
3 February	TC2282	1 February	TC7776	1 November	TD/4124
10 February	TC2341	25 February	TC8038	30 November	TD/4724
5 March	TC2342	3 March	TC8039	1 December	TD/4725
31 March	TC2490	31 March	TC8335	22 December	TD/5169
1 April	TC2491	1 April	TC8336		
30 April	TC2681	28 April	TC8571	**1951**	
1 May	TC2662	2 May	TC8572	1 January	TD/5170
30 May	TC2881	31 May	TC8858	31 January	TD/5799
2 June	TC2882	1 June	TC8859	2 February	TD/5800
30 June	TC3101	31 June	TC9127	28 February	TD/6391
2 July	TC3102	1 July	TC9128	1 March	TD/6392
24 July	TC3281	22 July	TC9329	30 March	TD/6948
11 August	TC3282	8 August	TC9330	3 April	TD/6949
29 August	TC3451	31 August	TC9566	27 April	TD/7467
1 September	TC3452	1 September	TC9567	1 May	TD/7468
30 September	TC3681	31 September	TC9845	31 May	TD/8081
1 October	TC3682	3 October	TC9846	1 June	TD/8042
30 October	TC3951	27 October	TC10065	29 June	TD/8701
3 November	TC3952	1 November	TC10066	2 July	TD/8702
26 November	TC4171	29 November	TC10251	26 July	TD/9362
1 December	TC4172			13 August	TD/9363
31 December	TC4411			31 August	TD/9928
				3 September	TD/9929
				28 September	TD/10654

October: TD/10655 was produced on 4 October, although TD/1056 started on 1 October. Month finished on 31 October with TD/11322.

1 November	TD/11323
30 November	TD/12100
3 December	TD/12101
20 December	TD/12577

1952

1 January	TD/12580
2 January	TD/12578 – TD12579
31 January	TD/13374
1 February	TD/13375
28 February	TD/14064
3 March	TD/14065
31 March	TD/14797
1 April	TD/14798
30 April	TD/15561
1 May	TD/15562
30 May	TD/16746
4 June	TD/16747
30 June	TD/17647
1 July	TD/17647
25 July	TD/18606

August: it appears that the factory's annual holiday during this period was the first two weeks of August)

11 August	TD/18607
29 August	TD/19345
1 September	TD/19346
30 September	TD/30433
1 October	TD/20434
31 October	TD/21576
3 November	TD/21577
28 November	TD/22612
1 December	TD/22613
31 December	TD/23634

1953

1 January	TD/23635
30 January	TD/24631
2 February	TD/24632
27 February	TD/25623
2 March	TD/25624
31 March	TD/26487
1 April	TD/26488
30 April	TD/27285
1 May	TD/27286
29 May	TD/28127
3 June	TD/28128
30 June	TD/28964
1 July	TD/28965
24 July	TD/29723
10 August	TD/29724
17 August	TD/29915

TF

On 12 May 1953, prototype chassis number 0250, engine number XPAG/TD3/26849, was produced. On 12 August the second prototype 0251 was produced, engine number XPAG/TD2/29748, and full production started on 17 September with chassis number HGA13/501, progressing to chassis number HDB46/574 on 28 September.

1953

5 October	HDP46/575
29 October	HDE43/901
3 November	HDE43/902
30 November	HDB26/1419
2 December	HDB26/1420
31 December	HDE43/2177

1954

4 January	HDE43/2178
28 January	HDC46/2942
1 February	HDC46/2943
26 February	HDP26/3625
2 March	HDP26/3626
31 March	HDA46/4552
2 April	HDA16/4553
30 April	HDE23/5226
3 May	HDE23/5227
31 May	HDC46/5946

TF 1500 production commenced on 13 July 1954 and the 1500 was then made in batches between TF6501-6550, TF6751-6850, TF6951-10100, this being the last TF produced, on 4 April 1955. Interspersed with these cars, between June 1954 and April 1955, were 1250s. For instance, on 3 January 1955 chassis numbers 8571-8575 were produced, but from this point on production dates become obscure, though chassis number 8644 was made on 4 January 1955 and 10100 on 4 April 1955.

Casting Numbers

There are numbers on the cylinder blocks and cylinder heads which some uninitiated people have often confused with production dates, but close examination clearly indicates that this is not the case. They are in fact casting numbers, and can be found on the left-hand side of the block.

The 1250 XPAG engine had the casting number 24146 embossed on it. When I bought my first TC, which was registered in October 1946, I saw this casting number on the block and assumed it had been made on 24 January 1946! This casting remained unchanged throughout the production of the TB, the TC and the TD, as well as the Y-types, until 1952, when the round-hole block was introduced as described earlier. By the time the T-type and TD had arrived, the water drain tap on the block, which was originally behind the exhaust manifold on the earlier XPAG engines, was moved to the front of the block on the right-hand side, just behind the bearer plate. Its appearance also changed in that it looked more like a tap than the previous one behind the manifold, which was rather like a butterfly valve.

In July 1950 at engine number XPAG/TD/2985 the block casting was slightly changed as the plinth holding the oil filter clamp was made slightly bigger to accommodate a third securing bolt. The casting number then changed to 24445. The changes in 1952 when the round-hole block was introduced signalled another change in the casting number to 168421. The extra digit clearly indicates that this is not a date!

Just to confuse things, a bit later in 1952, when the clamping for the distributor was changed, the block was changed again - in fact the top surface on which the distributor sits was lowered by approximately *1/8in and the boss holding the set screw on the earlier distributors had to be removed with the provision of a side boss for the cotter bolt, but the block casting number was not changed.

In 1954, when the TF1500 appeared, it had a completely new cylinder block and the casting number became AEF117.

The cylinder heads similarly had casting numbers on them. The number is found on the top of the right-hand side of the cylinder head. The number on the early XPAG cylinder head with the banana-shaped water holes was 22952 and this remained unchanged until 1952, when the round-holed cylinder head, casting number 168422, was introduced. This cylinder head was later slightly changed, an undercut being introduced below the inlet and exhaust valve seats. The undercut was in the opposite direction to the ports but it does mean that if you are fitting larger inlet valves, this head is not as efficient as the 22952 cylinder head. The earlier heads are superior when gas-flowed and polished. The 168422 head remained basically unchanged. The big-valve cylinder head used on the TD Mark II and all 1250cc TFs bears the number 168425.

The TF 1500 cylinder head carried the casting number AEF118 as, like the block, the water passages were moved and of course the TF cylinder head had to be made to match. It is therefore very important when fitting cylinder head gaskets that you have the right water hole spacings.

It will be noted that the numbers have different arrangements. The original five-digit number was a Morris Motors casting number, but when the British Motor Corporation was formed all the MG part numbers were changed and had the prefix 168. Later on in the mid-1950s, as BMC consolidated, the part numbers for the T-series were again changed to an AE prefix. This is noticeable in the numbering of crankshafts, for instance: the early crankshafts had a five-digit number, whereas the later ones, made with better steel, were numbered 168557. This could perhaps be better illustrated by comparing the numbers given to the various camshafts. The original TC camshaft was first coded MG862/171 and then X24084, but by the 1950s, if you wanted a new one the part number was AAA5776 - the same as for the early TD engines. When the new camshaft was introduced for the XPAG engines in 1952 it had the part number 168553, which was later coded AAA3096, and this of course was the same in the later TD and TFs. There were also hotted-up camshafts available from the special tuning division. What was described as a three-quarter race camshaft was coded AEG122, while the full-race camshaft was numbered 168551, becoming AAA3095 in later life. From this it may be deduced that the three-quarter race camshaft AEG122 was introduced fairly late in XPAG production as it had one of the later numbers, whereas the 168551 full-race camshaft originated from an earlier time.

XPAG/XPEG Engine modifications

The author is indebted to Roger Wilson for permission to reproduce this information.

The dates given are the installation dates in the production records for the engines stated. However, it must be noted that although engines were numbered consecutively, they were not fitted into cars in the same order, often days or weeks out of sequence. Even the "first" engine for each type was not, except for the TB, installed in each first production car (Y type uncertain, see later note), but they were all installed on the respective first days of production. In addition, prototype vehicles usually had engines from other series. The early Y type production records have been lost, so dates are only available from the 31-8-51 onwards.

Engine No.
XPAG/501
1/5 1939
Introduction of the XPAG engine in the TB using the 11/57/52/24/.019"/.315" lift camshaft coded MG862/171 (later coded X24084, then AAA 5576). Block casting no 24142, then 24146 (design unchanged, both with "MG" logo), head casting no 22952.

XPAG/883
17-9-45
Introduction of the TC engine. Timing chain tensioner introduced, can be fitted to earlier engines. NB: XPAG/883 was never fitted to a TB, despite its appearance in the TA/TB parts list. The production records indicate that it was fitted to TC chassis 0262, which is neither the prototype nor the first production car. Block and head castings unchanged.

XPAG/2020
17-9-46
Aluminium rocker cover introduced.

XPAG/2966
19-3-47
Aluminium rocker cover deleted.

XPAG/SC/10001
1946 or 1947
Introduction of the Y type engine, with the 11/57/52/24/.019"/.256" lift camshaft coded MG900/106. The block drain valve was moved forward, and a short tube introduced for the dipstick, requiring a slightly longer dipstick than for the TC. In addition, the sharp "kink" in the tappet inspection cover breather pipe was removed, and the block to head oil pipe was altered so that the hose take-off was directly from the bottom banjo, thus not using the TB/TC hollow securing bolt. The rocker cover oil filler was also moved from the rear (TB/TC) to the front, putting it rather close to the water temperature sensor capillary tube. Block and head castings unchanged.

XPAG/SC/13404
Dipstick and tube increased in length. However, according to the parts list, the YT engines (with TB/TC camshaft and twin carbs. etc) had the longer dipstick and tube from when they were introduced at XPAG/TL/11604 and XPAG/TR12026 (engine numbers from SC series). Despite this, it is known that many early YTs still had short dipsticks and tubes, possibly to use up already assembled engines.

XPAG/TD/501
10-11-49
XPAG/SC/14023
Introduction of the TD engine, with the moved block drain valve and oil filler, altered breather pipe, longer dipstick and tube plus banjo fitting on the oil pump outlet pipe (see next item). The block to head oil pipe was left as for the TB/TC, but inverted, putting the gauge take-off at the head end. In addition, for both TD and SC engines, the starter ring and pinion were modified - 93/10 prior to change, 120/9 after. However, the starter ring internal diameter was unchanged, so the later 120/9 arrangement, with smaller starter motor, could be fitted onto a TB, TC or early Y flywheel. Block and head castings unchanged.

XPAG/SC/14083
The method of securing the oil pump outlet pipe was changed from a 2 bolt flanged end fitting on the pump body to a banjo fitting on the pump end plate.
This means that the pump and outlet pipe are a matched pair. Also, according to the parts lists, both the T-type and YT had the banjo fitting from the start.

XPAG/TD/2985
26-7-50
XPAG/SC/15405
Purolater oil filter PTX346 (MG part 162438) replaced the original Wilmot Breedon filter (MG part X22768). The clamp straps were widened and changed from 2

bolt fixing to 3 bolts; thus the pad on the block was enlarged to have 3 tapped holes (2 in the same position as before), but the later oil filter does fit both clamps. New block casting no 24445 (with "MG" logo), head casting unchanged.

XPAG/TD/7576
Different shaped piston skirt used, bringing in line with the TD type.

XPAG/TD/6483)
1-3-51
XPAG/SC/16463
Modified water pump introduced, fitted with integral seal. Can be fitted to older engines. Original no longer available. NB: The *Motor Trader* 1952 service data leaflet for the TD gives engine number 6482, which must be wrong.

XPAG/TD/7576
11-4-51
XPAG/SC/16729
The position of the oil suction filter in the sump was moved to a central position to give better pick-up (particularly on left-hand bends). The parts can be fitted to older sumps.

XPAG/TD/9008
4-7-51
XPAG/SC/16831
Exhaust valve rockers, square to shaft, had the bosses and bushes lengthened (to match inlet rockers) to reduce rocker shaft wear. The shaft was lengthened and washers were put at both ends of each spring, also shortened, to reduce friction. The inletrockers were unchanged.

XPAG/SC/16831
Camshaft design changed to give quieter running and more torque. Coded X22329 (later AAA5594), the timing was 5/45/45/5/.0199V.315" lift, and was the same as used for the XPJM/XPJW engines. The camshaft was not used for YT engines.

XPAG/TD2/9408
18-7-51
XPAG/SC2/16916
The engine code was altered at this point to indicate the fitting of the 8" diameter clutch. Bellhousings fitted to engines prior to this have a 5/8" clutch fork shaft. From this number the bellhousings have a 3/4" clutch fork shaft, moved back 7mm to accommodate the 8" clutch. The bellhousing back-to-front distance was not changed, and the thrust bearing was the same. The flywheel was also changed to have a larger clutch face, and the starter ring had its internal diameter increased (although the ratio was still 120/9 with the same starter motor). The engines and transmission units were supposedly non-interchangeable. NB: For some unknown reason the T type production records do not start mentioning "TD2" until the 3/9/52, almost 2 months after the change, when engine numbers were approx.10200 and above. As already mentioned, the early Y type records have been lost. However, the records for the 31-8-51 onwards only show "SC2", and are for engine numbers approx. 16934 and above; thus the missing records probably started showing "SC2" at the correct time. In addition, the Y type block to head oil pipe was adopted for the TD, putting the gauge take-off at the gallery end.

XPAG/SC2/17131
21-11-51
This was the first engine in a YB, and YB engines generally went from this number upwards. However, one earlier engine, XPAG/SC2/17100 (not 16916 as per the YB parts list), was also installed in a YB, and some higher number engines had already been installed in the last few Y-types.

XPAG/TD2/14224
22-2-52
XPAG/SC2/17293
1-4-52
A modified oil pump was introduced, with a replacement element oil filter. The pump can be fitted to earlier engines, but some modifications are required. These were detailed in an early copy of the T Register bulletin, but Blower also helps. The block part number was also changed from SA2404/9 to SA2404/10. NB: The mention, in the 1958 TD parts list, of this SA2404/10 block being introduced at XPAG/TD/9404 owing only to a change in oil bypass plug is very strange, and seems to be an error. The 9404 would appear to be wrong as it is only recorded for the new plug and block, which had no physical changes at that time. The new pump (the reason for the change in block suffix from /9 to /10) is correctly listed as being introduced at XPAG/TD2/14224.

XPAG/TD2/14948
2-4-52
XPAG/SC2/17383
13-6-52
A larger, 10½ pint finned aluminium sump was introduced (MG part 168137). This can be fitted to earlier

engines. NB: The earlier sumps had a step in their depth at the front, which was eliminated on the larger sumps. This makes an engine with an early sump much easier to lift out of a TD/TF chassis (and probably Y-type), as the front suspension crossmember does not get in the way. In addition, the oil suction filter was changed slightly and incorporated a strap, which was bolted to the sump baffle plate. However, the TD parts list indicates that these filter changes did not come in until XPAG/TD2/15372; the Y-type had the larger sump slightly later, so it had the changed filter from the start. The parts can be fitted to any sump, provided the baffle plate is cut and drilled appropriately. It is rather strange that neither the TD nor the YB parts list mentions the new sump, although they do show the change in baffle plate.

XPAG/TD2/15 861
12-5-52
XPAG/SC2/17392
25-6-52
Clutch plate linings with a higher frictional coefficient were introduced. The original specification is no longer available. Applies to both 7¼" and 8" clutches.

XPAG/TD3/17029
9-6-52
Applied, in June 1952, to a Mark II engine with the coding changed from TD2 to TD3, and according to the 1958 parts list signified the introduction of a new cylinder head assembly SA2203/11. As the /11 suffix is 1 greater than for the SA2203/10 round water hole head assembly to be introduced at XPAG/TD2/22735 and XPAG/SC2/17994, this implies that the Mark II now had the round water hole head (but not the block) well in advance of the TD or YB. The suffix change from /10 to /11 would be a consequence of larger valves being fitted for the Mark II. Prior to this the Mark II heads had not been given a specific part number. In addition, the following Mark II engines with lower numbers were installed after the above engine (because MG did not install engines in numerical order), and the production records indicate that they were also given the TD3 coding: 16208, 16266, 16559, 16580, 16581, 16626, 16631, 16636, 16927, 17003, 17007 and 17028. The parts list does not make it clear, but it is probable that they were fitted with the new round water hole head assemblies. New head casting no 168422.

XPAG/TD2/17298
4-6-52
XPAG/SC2/17432
12-6-52
Shorter pushrods (MG part 168431) and longer adjusting screws (MG part X21231) were fitted to the valve gear. They can be fitted to older engines. For skimmed heads, the best combination is short pushrods and short screws (and no plates under the rocker posts) for a slight reduction in valve gear weight. Even better to combine this with reducing the length of the inner valve spring sleeves (must not be omitted) plus extra oil seals at the tops of the inlet guides.

XPAG/TD2/17969
9-7-52
XPAG/SC2/17463
22-7-52
A new cylinder block (MG part SA. 2404/11, later AEG5) was introduced, with improved cooling and round water passage holes, to match the round water hole head already on the Mark II (and due to be introduced for all engines). The "MG" logo was lost, and all blocks now had a Wolseley "W" logo. A new gasket (MG part no. X24481), still with oval water holes, was introduced, and the original deleted. The Mark II may have had this block slightly earlier (as Blower implies) at XPAG/TD3/17029 when the TD3 coding was introduced, but it is not clear from the parts lists. New block casting no 168421 (with "W" logo).

XPAG/TD2/18291)
8-7-52
XPAG/SC2/17500)
20-8-52
The material specification for the exhaust valves was altered, original specification no longer available.

XPAG/TD2/20942)
6-10-52
XPAG/SC2/17670)
6-10-52
A cotter bolt fixing for the distributor was introduced (which cannot be fitted to earlier engines), but according to the MG parts lists for both cars, there was no change of distributor. However, the upper machined surface on which the distributor rests was lowered by approx ⅛" which puts the drive gear for the earlier distributors (either DKY4A or DKYH4A) below the position to mesh correctly with the camshaft gear (although they still do mesh together). To correct this, the distributor would need spacer rings to put the gears in the correct position, but there is no mention of

the introduction of spacer rings in the parts lists. Thus the later D2A4 distributors, which have shorter stems, must have been introduced at this time. In addition, data supplied many years ago by Lucas Parts and Service Dept to Chip Old, Technical Rep. for the New England MG T Register, allowing him to prepare distributor parts lists, also indicated that the distributor change occurred at this point; ie when the cotter bolt fixing was introduced. NB: It is strange that MG did not introduce a new part number (and block casting number) for what was to some extent a new block, as they did change the part number when only the dipstick tube or oil bypass plug were changed. However, neither the TD (including the Mark II, for which the parts list does not even mention the cotter bolt fixing) nor the YB part lists indicates any change in engine part number at this time. Block casting number apparently unchanged at 168421.

XPAG/TD2/20972
6-10-52
XPAG/SC2/17670
6-10-52
The end plate of the oil pump was fitted with a special priming plug at the top. The plate can be fitted to most oil pumps (not "banjo" pumps), or the modification can be done to any oil pump after engine no. XPAG/TD2/14224 and XPAG/SC2/17293 (it may even be possible to modify "banjo" pumps).

XPAG/TD2/22717
25-11-52
Clutch cable changed to rod (and a worthwhile conversion for earlier cars). Not adopted for the YB.

XPAG/TD2/22735
26-11-52
XPAG/SC2/17994
6-2-53
A modified cylinder head (already on the Mark II), with improved cooling and round water passage holes, was introduced. This cylinder head (MG part SA.2203/10) requires ¾" thread length spark plugs, as opposed to ½" thread length on all earlier heads. Although for the Mark II, MG changed the engine coding to TD3 for the introduction of this head, they made no change to the TD2 or SC2 codings for the introduction of the same head. Any XPAG head can be used with any XPAG block, but if a round water passage block is used with a round water passage head, then a new head gasket (MG part 168423) with round water holes, introduced at this time, should be used. Any other combination must use an oval hole gasket. In addition, the side ports in the head were supposedly made larger (I have one of each cylinder head, and it does appear correct), with the manifold gasket altered to suit. In any event, the "copper" asbestos gaskets, and some of the metal/fibre gaskets, overlap into all the ports of my round water hole cylinder head, whereas the Octagon Car Club TD/TF gaskets do not. New head casting number 168422.

XPAG/TD3/22978)
1-12-52
Compression ratio of Mark II reduced from 8.6:1 to 8.1:1. However, the following Mark II engines with lower numbers were installed after the above engine number: 22309, 22891, 22899, 22901, 22905, 22909, 22911, 22943, 22950, 22971 and 22977, but presumably have 8.1:1 compression ratio. Also, Mark II engine 22980 (a higher number) was installed before 22978, and therefore may still have 8.6:1 compression ratio. Better to check head depths (head assembly part number apparently unchanged)!

XPAG/TD2/24116
5-1-53
XPAG/SC2/18097
17-3-53
A new common camshaft was introduced, timing 5/45/45/5/.012"/.327" lift, coded 168553 (later AAA3096). Also fitted in conjunction with the camshaft was a new cylinder head (rocker) cover assembly (MG part SA2407/5) with a new .012" valve clearance brass plate (MG part 162279). These parts are not essential (although desirable) should one wish to use one of these camshafts.

XPAG/TD2/24489
14-1-53
XPAG/TD3/26744
25-3-53
XPAG/SC2/18097
17-3-53
According to the parts lists, this is the point when the distributor model was changed from either DKY4A or DKYH4A to D2A4. However, this is questionable - see comments earlier at XPAG/TD2/20942 and XPAG/SC2/17670 when cotter bolt clamping was introduced.

XPAG/TD2/26364
13-3-53
XPAG/SC2/18097
17-3-53
A new oil suction filter was fitted to the sump to prevent loss of oil pressure on deceleration. It was

basically a modified housing, with a forward facing scoop to pick up the oil from the front of the sump; however, it had the opposite effect during acceleration. The filter can be fitted to all 10½ pint sumps.

XPAG/TD2/26635
30-3-53
XPAG/SC2/18120
24-3-53
A new type of oil pump body was introduced with increased oil level, which enabled the pump to be kept primed. The pump can be fitted to any engine (with mods), as detailed in an early copy of the T Register bulletin, but the Blower manual also helps.

XPAG/TD2/27551
24-4-53
XPAG/SC2/18272
22-5-53
New crankshaft fitted, made from EN.100 steel. MG part 168557, actually on the crankshaft! NB: Parts list gives numbers dependent on whether the Oilite bush was fitted, if the crank was ground undersize, or if bearings were supplied. Original steel specification no longer available.

XPAG/TD2/27867
8-5-53
XPAG/TD3/27996
13-5-53
XPAG/SC2/19037
Prior to these engine numbers the valve guides were pressed in until .945" protruded. From these numbers on valve guides must protrude .964". This is because the depth of the valve spring counterbore was increased by .5mm to ensure that the valve springs do not become coil bound with the new camshaft introduced at XPAG/TD2/24116 and XPAG/SC2/18097. For present owners to check which cylinder head they have, I have measured a .964" projection head (never reconditioned) and the depth from the rocker pedestal face to the counterbore at its shallowest (close to the pedestal) is .073"; thus earlier heads should measure .053". MG may have been over concerned about this point, as I run a .945" projection head (shallow counterbores) with a Crane camshaft, which has .339" inlet valve lift, yet the valve springs do not become coil bound. However, I use 120lb valve springs, so a problem could occur with 150lb springs as they have extra turns; thus the concern may only have been for the TD Mark II.

XPAG/TF/31943
30-12-53
The heads of the bolts for the gearbox remote control were drilled for locking wire. This is unimportant if wide spring washers are used and the correct torque is applied. Not applicable to the YB.

XPAG/TF/30301
17-9-53
Introduction of the TF engine, the only modifications being the reduction in cylinder head depth to increase compression ratio to 8.1:1, boring out the valve chokes for larger valves, plus larger carburettors, as for the TD Mark II. Can be done to any cylinder head, (and useful to omit any plates under the rocker posts). Block casting no 168421 (with "W" logo), new head casting no 168425.

XPAG/TF/31263
9-11-53
The oil pump was modified by drilling a 3.5mm bleed hole in the priming plug to make the pump self-priming. Older pumps from XPAG/TD2/14224 or XPAG/SC2/17293 can have this modification done, see Blower manual.

XPAG/TF/31943)
30-12-53
The lower banjo coupling on the oil pipe, gallery to head, had the internal diameter reduced to .055". Can be fitted to earlier engines. However, at least for the later longer rocker shaft, the valve gear is still over-lubricated, and I have reduced this hole to .040" (1mm) with no problems, although it does put slightly more oil to the rear main bearing.

XPAG/TF/33024
8-2-54
Modified sump fitted; flange on oil pick-up pipe secured to sump by 4 bolts as compared to 2 previously (although 2 in same positions as before).

XPEG/501
22-7-54
Introduction of the XPEG 1466cc engine in the TF1500. New block casting no AEF117 (with "W" logo), new head casting no AEF118.

Bibliography

Before listing out in full all my sources, those of you who do not own a copy of *TCs Forever* by Michael Sherrell are recommended to try and acquire one. It is the definitive book on the TC and because it is devoted to just that model is a major reference source a book like this can't hope to mirror. Also on the TC, if you can lay your hands on a back copy of *Road and Track* from April 1983 do read The Editor's account of a long journey in a TC in Eastern USA. Entitled *The Great TC Trek* it is a magical account of being in one of these cars for several days, driving and enjoying them in the way they were designed for.

The MG Workshop Manual	W.R.Blower 1952-1964 edition.	Motor Racing Publications
Tuning and Maintenance of MGs	Philip H. Smith	G,T.Foulis and Co.Ltd
British Sports Cars	Gregor Grant 1958 edition	G.T. Foulis and Co Ltd
The Story of The MG Sports Car	Wilson McComb 1973 edition	J.M.Dent and Son Ltd
The Immortal T Series	Chris Harvey 1977	The Oxford Illustrated Press Ltd
TCs Forever	Michael Sherrell 1990	Published and distributed by the Author
The T Series Handbook	The New England MG T Register	
MG Cars 1948-1951		Brooklands Book Company
MG Cars.1952-1954.		Brooklands Book Company
The BMC Competitions Department	Bill Price	Haynes Publishing Group
The Magic of MG	Mike Allison. 1972	Dalton Watson Ltd
Original MG T Series	Anders Clausager	Bay View Books

MG Car Club T Register Bulletins and Newsletters-1963-2004. In their various forms!
TA Owners Handbook.
TC Owners Handbook.
M.G. TD/TF Workshop Manual.
TA/TB Parts List.
TC Parts List.
The MG Octagon Car Club Bulletins.
Safety Fast! The Magazine of the MG Car Club.
The MG Car Club T-Register and Roger Wilson in particular for the Appendix "XPAG Engine Modifications."

Unless otherwise stated the Photographs are from the Author's personal collection, The Publisher's collection and from the Archives of the MG Car Club and the T-Register.